WALKING

ALSTON &
ALLENDALE

HILLSIDE GUIDES - ACROSS THE NORTH AND BEYOND

The Uplands of Britain - full colour hardback books
- THE HIGH PEAKS OF ENGLAND & WALES
- YORKSHIRE DALES, MOORS & FELLS

Hillwalking - Lake District
- LAKELAND FELLS - SOUTH
- LAKELAND FELLS - NORTH
- LAKELAND FELLS - EAST
- LAKELAND FELLS - WEST

Long Distance Walks
- COAST TO COAST WALK
- DALES WAY
- CLEVELAND WAY
- WESTMORLAND WAY
- FURNESS WAY
- LADY ANNE'S WAY
- BRONTE WAY
- CALDERDALE WAY
- PENDLE WAY
- CALDERDALE WAY
- NIDDERDALE WAY
- TRANS-PENNINE WAY

Circular Walks - Yorkshire Dales
- WHARFEDALE
- MALHAMDALE
- SWALEDALE
- NIDDERDALE
- THREE PEAKS COUNTRY
- WENSLEYDALE
- HOWGILL FELLS

Circular Walks - Peak District
- NORTHERN PEAK
- CENTRAL PEAK
- EASTERN PEAK
- SOUTHERN PEAK
- WESTERN PEAK

Circular Walks - Lancashire
- BOWLAND
- PENDLE & THE RIBBLE
- WEST PENNINE MOORS

Circular Walks - North Pennines
- TEESDALE
- EDEN VALLEY
- ALSTON & ALLENDALE

Circular Walks - North York Moors
- WESTERN MOORS
- SOUTHERN MOORS

Circular Walks - South Pennines
- ILKLEY MOOR
- CALDERDALE
- BRONTE COUNTRY
- SOUTHERN PENNINES

WayMaster Visitor Guides
- YORKSHIRE DALES

---

*Send for a detailed current catalogue and price list
and also visit www.hillsidepublications.co.uk*

WALKING COUNTRY

ALSTON &
ALLENDALE

Paul Hannon

Hillside

HILLSIDE
PUBLICATIONS
12 Broadlands
Shann Park
Keighley
West Yorkshire
BD20 6HX

First published 2004

© Paul Hannon 2004

ISBN 1 870141 77 6

Cover illustration: Featherstone Bridge, South Tyne
Back cover: Above Nenthead; Alston; Allenmill Chimney
Page One: Limestone Brae, West Allen Dale
Page Three: Carving, East Allen Dale
(Paul Hannon/Hillslides Picture Library)

The sketch maps in this book are based upon
1947 Ordnance Survey One-Inch maps

Printed in Great Britain by
Carnmor Print
95-97 London Road
Preston
Lancashire
PR1 4BA

CONTENTS

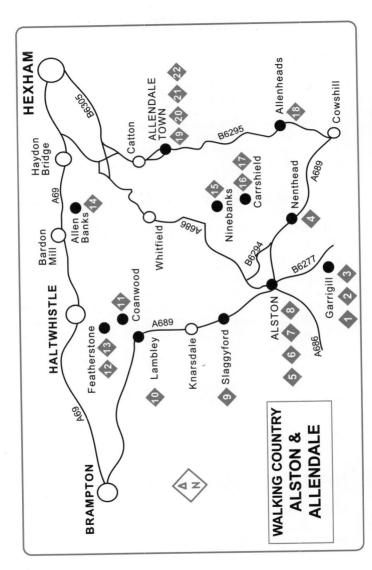

WALKING COUNTRY
ALSTON &
ALLENDALE

6

INTRODUCTION

The North Pennines form England's largest Area of Outstanding Natural Beauty, reaching from Stainmore, on the edge of the Yorkshire Dales National Park, north to the Tyne Gap, on the edge of Northumberland National Park. AONB status came as recently as 1988, and only after much wrangling - it wasn't so much that local people didn't think their area beautiful, just that there were those who didn't want all and sundry drawn here to enjoy it! The North Pennines divides into very individual areas, loosely based upon the Pennine watershed which forms the spine along the west of the area, and also shelters the Eden Valley beneath its steep western flanks. The major valleys radiate spoke-like from Teesdale in the south, round via Weardale, the Derwent Valley, Allendale and South Tynedale.

The parallel valleys of South Tynedale and Allendale are very similar in character and form a logical group for the purposes of this book. Both run from south to north, and just short of the great line of Hadrian's mighty frontier, the South Tyne swings east to be swelled below Bardon Mill by the Allen. The Allen is formed by the meeting of the West Allen and East Allen rivers, both little more than moorland burns until they merge. Within this book's area the deep valleys run between high and lonely moorlands, frequented only by occasional walkers and grouse shooting parties. Some of England's highest roads traverse the open moortops to link the daleheads with each other as well as the neighbouring Tees, Wear and Eden dales.

The small market town of Alston sits at the heart of South Tynedale, and makes the perfect focal point for this collection of walks. This area was not always as peaceful as you find it today, and although it had been mined since pre-Roman times, it was the lead mining boom of the 18th and 19th centuries that made virtually the entire region a scene of great activity and industry. As labour-intensive lead mining dominated everything, the population was naturally much greater. Though the industry largely halted over a century ago, evidence abounds in the remains of mines, smelt mills with dramatic moortop chimneys, shafts, levels and spoil heaps. Please be warned: it is extremely dangerous to go casually wandering into old mine levels and adits, most have remained untouched for decades and they are notoriously unsafe.

Several villages now feature heritage centres where great initiative has preserved some of the lead mining past to give a much clearer picture of what went on here, not that very long ago.

That elder statesman of long distance trails the Pennine Way passes through the western edge of the area, travelling the full length of South Tynedale to link the major landmarks of Cross Fell and Hadrian's Wall. Over a millennium and a half earlier, the Romans marched a similar line from the Eden to the Wall, and both routes are explored in these walks. Within these pages you will find yourself among woodland, riverbank, stately parkland, heather moors, old railways, country lanes, ancient fieldpaths and byways; wide panoramas, welcoming villages. All take you through scenes of great beauty and tranquillity, history and grandeur.

Using the guide

Each walk is self contained, with essential information being followed by a concise route description and simple map. Dovetailed in between are notes and illustrations of features along the way. Snippets of information have been placed in *italics* to ensure that the essential route description is easier to locate. The sketch maps serve to identify the location of the routes rather than the fine detail, and whilst the description should be sufficient to guide you around, an Ordnance Survey map is strongly recommended.

To gain the most from a walk, the detail of the 1:25,000 scale Explorer maps is unsurpassed. They also serve to vary walks as desired, giving an improved picture of your surroundings and the availability of linking paths. Just two maps cover the walks in this book:

- Explorer OL31 - North Pennines (Teesdale & Weardale)
- Explorer OL43 - Hadrian's Wall

Also very useful for general planning are two Landranger maps at the scale of 1:50,000:

- 86, Haltwhistle & Brampton
- 87, Hexham & Haltwhistle

Milestone, Alston

ALSTON is a hugely interesting little town, claiming - along with Buxton in Derbyshire - to be England's highest market town. Certainly the upper part of town easily breaches the 1000ft barrier. Standing above the South Tyne at its confluence with the smaller Nent, Alston is almost entirely surrounded by moorland, wild and seemingly always windswept. Mention of the Tyne is a clue to Alston's unique situation, for this is the only town in Cumbria to stand east of the Pennine watershed. In all respects Alston's loyalties tend more to the North-east than the North-west: its inclusion in Cumberland seems almost the result of an outrageous administrative blunder in days gone by, or perhaps more likely in modern times?

The town perches on a steep hillside east of the river, and the focal point is the cobbled main street which climbs to the top of town and is lined by interesting buildings. At the bottom stands the Town Hall with its excellent information centre, and across the road, slightly back, is St Augustine's parish church dating only from 1869. The street widens to incorporate the small market place, wherein stands a well-known landmark, the Market Cross of 1765. This large structure, a popular focal gathering point, has suffered demolition by runaway lorry but returned fully restored. Ranged behind it, the area known as The Butts contains some of Alston's oldest buildings: set just around the back is the sizeable High Mill, which dates from 1767.

A pleasing feature is the seemingly disproportionate number of pubs, an indication of the town's greater importance in mining times, and also its remoteness from any equally sizeable community. Half a dozen are ranged the length of the street: be sure to plan any tour from the top! Tearooms and fish & chip shops also feature, with other shops ranging from the practical to the absorbing, including a fascinating multi-roomed second-hand bookshop. Alston youth hostel is a crucial staging post on the Pennine Way, and there is a campsite. Other features of interest include the fire station in the tiny Old Grammar School; a Friends' Meeting House of 1732; the tiny Roman Catholic church of St Wulstan; and the Hub Museum by the station.

Alston was on the railway network as recently as 1976, when the single-track branch from Haltwhistle was closed. Through the efforts of enthusiasts the Victorian station has been restored and a section of line re-opened. Now narrow gauge rather than standard, its near Toytown appearance is no detriment to the attraction of seeing trains back in the South Tyne valley.

THE CORPSE ROAD

START *Garrigill*   *Grid ref.* **NY 744415**

DISTANCE *5¹⁄₂ miles (9km)*

ORDNANCE SURVEY MAPS
1:50,000
Landranger 86 - Haltwhistle & Brampton **or**
Landranger 87 - Hexham & Haltwhistle
Landranger 91 - Appleby-in-Westmorland (tiny section)
1:25,000
Explorer OL31 - North Pennines (Teesdale/Weardale)

ACCESS *Start from the village centre. Ample roadside parking (not on the green). Served by bus from Alston.*

> *A moderately wild walk based on an ancient trans-Pennine track on the flanks of Cross Fell. While you reach 1850ft above sea level, you already start at well over a thousand feet up!*

For a note on Garrigill see page 16. Leave the village green by the road at the south-western corner, a no-through-road signed to Tynehead. Passing the church on the left, leaving the houses behind you come to a cluster of buildings at Gatehead, featuring a Primitive Methodist Chapel of 1885. Leave the road and turn right past the chapel, the way continuing as a firm, unsurfaced track rising between walls. *This is the Corpse Road, so named as this was the route by which the deceased of Garrigill were taken for burial at Kirkland in the Eden Valley prior to having their own consecrated ground. In use up to the 17th century, this 11-mile crossing of the Pennine watershed attained 2575ft/785m as it negotiated the northern edge of Cross Fell: harsh winter conditions must have tested the funeral parties' resolve! The entire section used on this walk was given its considerably firmer surface to facilitate access to lead mines high on Cross Fell's flank, notably the large Cashwell Mine. The old way immediately offers good views back over village and valley.*

The gradients ease as the track swings right, then left to begin a near level section. Towards the end of this it rises gently to another right-hand bend. Leave at this point by taking a gate in the wall on the left. A grassy track heads across the moor, rising gently but fading before reaching a line of shooting butts. Now turn rather more steeply uphill, passing through the four-square stone butts amid patches of heather, and aim for a distinct gateway in the sky-line wall ahead. Passing through the scant line of an old wall, the hitherto moist going improves to enjoy a pathless slant up moor grass and heather to the gateway. *Ahead is a big wild country, with Cross Fell's long flat plateau top directly ahead.*

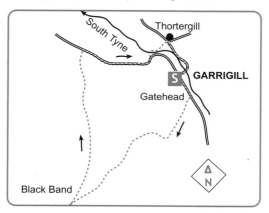

With the climbing virtually over, head away, initially level (crossing a grassy track) but then bear very slightly right. For the most part this is easy walking on grass between heathery tracts, gaining just a little height to angle towards the wall above, which hides the Corpse Road. Don't join the wall yet however, as towards the end you meet an intervening wall ascending from below. This is crossed by a gate in a section of fence, though the map suggests the gate should be at the top end of the fenced section, not the bottom. Thus if you're higher up, where you should be, simply step over the low fence confirmed by the presence of a faint trod. This runs to a gate in the wall just above, passing through to rejoin the Corpse Road. At around 1850ft/564m this is the summit of the walk, and a small pool makes a foreground to Cross Fell's great plateau top. *If tempted to make a visit, bear in mind it is still some five miles distant and more than a thousand feet higher, so don't go there unless suitably equipped for such an excursion.*

Turn right along the track to commence the return. It quickly passes through a gate/stile to become fully enclosed, which it remains all the way to Garrigill. After a splendid level section along Black Band the descent begins. *This brings magnificent views round from Melmerby Fell, across Hartside and around to Black Fell, also down the South Tyne valley to distant hills beyond parts of Alston. Garrigill itself also appears on the dale floor directly below.* Though you could also remain on the old road to rejoin the outward route further down, the full walk leaves it at a sharp bend to the right. Take the stile in front and slant right down the first of four rough enclosures, initially heathery, and largely unkempt and partly moist. Drop right to the bottom wall, where a stile awaits at a wall junction. Simply maintain this slant through an old wall, down to a ladder-stile in a wall, then down a reedy pasture to a stile/gate onto the Leadgate Road.

Turn right, and remain on this to run on and then down towards Garrigill. *During the steeper descent note a former chapel and graveyard in trees on the left.* The finish can be varied by taking a path on the left which runs the few steps to a bridge across the river. Across, turn right to accompany the lively South Tyne upstream, quickly emerging into a patch of open ground at the confluence of Garrigill Burn with the river. The path rises alongside this minor wooded gill to join a road at Low Houses Bridge. *Just short of the road it reveals a splendidly framed waterfall through the tall arch of the road bridge: at this point there is little to suggest that it is artificially enhanced! The road is joined opposite Beldy Chapel, a former Wesleyan Chapel of 1859. Also here is the entrance to Thortergill, a working blacksmith's forge with tearoom and waterfall walk (entrance fee payable).* Cross the bridge, noting the waterfall again, then simply continue along this road to re-enter the village centre by way of Garrigill Bridge.

2

SOUTH TYNE'S BANKS

START *Garrigill*   Grid ref. NY 744415

DISTANCE *5³4 miles (9km)*

ORDNANCE SURVEY MAPS
1:50,000
Landranger 86 - Haltwhistle & Brampton **or**
Landranger 87 - Hexham & Haltwhistle
1:25,000
Explorer OL31 - North Pennines (Teesdale/Weardale)

ACCESS *Start from the village centre. Ample roadside parking (not on the green). Served by bus from Alston.*

A beautiful, low level walk on both banks of the South Tyne, at its finest when the flowers of the meadows bloom in early summer

For a note on Garrigill, see page 16. Leave the charming green by heading north on the Leadgate road out of the village, the green tapering away as you leave by way of the isolated former school of 1850. Ignore two options to cross to a footbridge on the river, and just beyond, as the road starts to climb, take a gate/stile on the right (Pennine Way). A track heads away to a former mining site, currently an unsightly tip. A path passes round to the left, over a stream to a stile to escape into the first meadow, and what will now remain lovely surrounds.

At first the path ascends the minor bank in front. Running atop it the bank becomes wooded, then at the end slant back towards the river. On gaining the bank of the South Tyne a superb mile begins, soon to be happily confined by a wall on your left and delectable river scenery alongside. *In early summer a limitless supply of flower-rich meadow scenery blends idyllically with the river's charms: a lovely low waterfall is a top highlight.* Ultimately the path emerges into the open to reveal a footbridge across the river just ahead, a good place to take a break.

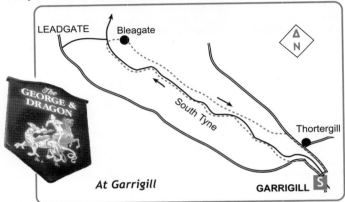

Don't cross but resume downstream on the west bank, largely pathless but remaining by the river. Through a step-stile beneath minor remains of lead mining spoil, cross a footbridge on a side-stream and shadow the river along two fieldsides, the second, longer one leading to a gateway at the far corner. A short track climbs into a field, but is quickly left by a wall-stile on the right to keep faith with the South Tyne. Across the next field a short enclosed section leads past a concrete ford on the river, beyond which wide flats open out. A thin path trends towards the river before reaching an area of scrub. While the path runs clearly on through this, the true right of way veers left, over a plank foot-bridge to a fence-stile into a field. A short section leads to a stile back to the end of the scrub, and along to another footbridge on another sidestream. Just ahead now is a bridge on the river. This one really is the walk's turning point, though first you might advance a few paces further to appreciate the major confluence of the Black Burn with the South Tyne, without doubt a location that merits a linger.

Cross the bridge and bear left up the steep little bank, with a good view of the confluence. Through a stile ascend the wallside to the farm at Bleagate. *Far across to the left rises the spire of Alston church.* At the top keep left of the outbuilding, through a gate into the yard, then turn up past the house to the end of a surfaced lane. At once turn right to a wall-stile across a tiny trickle, and begin the return half of the walk by heading along the wallside. *Big moorland views ahead feature the vast, sprawling flanks of the Cross Fell massif.* From the gate at the end cross a field centre, a nice path forming to drop towards renovated Low Sillyhall ahead. Passing through an intervening wall-stile the little path crosses to a gap well right of the buildings, then left atop the minor bank to a path junction. Keep left the few steps further to a stile/gate in a short kink of the wall, and head away along the field bottom with a wooded bank dropping away on your right. Passing through a pair of wall-stiles, keep straight on above the wooded bank.

This will remain your course pretty much all the way back. The way never strays more than a few paces from the bottom of the fields. Approaching the farm buildings at Low Craig, take a gate in front of the first barn and head on past the interesting range of buildings to the driveway. Don't follow it away, but go right a few paces to a stile in the facing wall, and resume as before away from the farm. The next field corner reveals a small spring as this smashing route continues to amble through a succession of meadows. With intervening stiles all in place, the way remains generally along the field bottoms as you pass beneath the renovated farmhouse at Middle Craig.

After gaining a little height, the path runs on to enter a small wooded gill, crossed by a footbridge and emerging into a contrastingly open scene. Ahead now is a fine prospect, looking beyond the river (including that opening mile) to the lonely dalehead beyond Garrigill. Follow the wall away above a minor bank, and pass through a gateway at the end. A sunken little path now slants left to a gate onto a road alongside a cemetery. Turn right on this quiet road back into Garrigill. At Low Houses Bridge is Beldy Chapel, a former Wesleyan Chapel of 1859. *Also here is the entrance to Thortergill, a working blacksmith's forge with a tearoom and waterfall walk (entrance fee).* Crossing the bridge here, note the artificially enhanced waterfall immediately upstream. The road leads on in the company of the South Tyne to suddenly swing right, crossing Garrigill Bridge to re-enter the village centre.

ASHGILL FORCE

START *Garrigill*   Grid ref. **NY 744415**

DISTANCE *3¹4 miles (5km)*

ORDNANCE SURVEY MAPS
1:50,000
Landranger 86 - Haltwhistle & Brampton **or**
Landranger 87 - Hexham & Haltwhistle
1:25,000
Explorer OL31 - North Pennines (Teesdale/Weardale)

ACCESS *Start from the village centre. Ample roadside parking (not on the green). Served by bus from Alston.*

> *The shortest walk in the book should not be dismissed: this is a delectable little ramble by the South Tyne, with the objective of a super waterfall in an atmospheric ravine*

Despite its lofty elevation at some 1085ft/330m Garrigill is a delightfully cosy village, the highest in the South Tyne valley, and hemmed in by high fell country. This old lead mining community is the sanctuary which Pennine Wayfarers seek after the long miles of Cross Fell. Set back from its broad greens are a fine range of cottages, and most importantly both the George & Dragon pub and a Post office/shop (tea/coffee to take out) with a stone flagged floor. There is a WC at the village hall and two quoits pitches on the green, while St John's church has a small bell-cote.

Leave the village green by the no-through-road at the south-western corner, signed to Tynehead. Passing the church on the left, leaving the houses behind you come to a cluster of buildings at Gatehead, featuring a Primitive Methodist Chapel of 1885, and the departure of the Pennine Way. Remain on the surfaced road which climbs away and runs on to pass Low Crossgill Farm. Here take a gate on the left and descend an inviting grassy way between walls. At the bottom is the stone arched Windshaw Bridge on the South Tyne. *The river is in splendid form as it channels its way through a dark gorge: in normal weather it is no more than a foot wide in places between the rocky walls and shelves.*

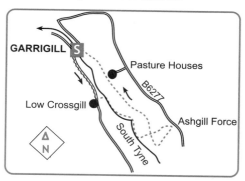

Across, leave the old lane and turn sharp right to accompany the river upstream. Passing through a kissing-gate, at once you encounter a notable confluence as Cross Gill comes in to double the South Tyne's youthful power. The path, never more than faint, accompanies the chirpy stream around several twists and turns, becoming enclosed towards the end on the edge of its tree-lined bank. An emphatic impasse is faced at a confluence with inflowing Ashgill Beck, a super moment as the latter is also within a gorge at this point. A stile sends you upstream with the side beck, a lovely little stroll to a footbridge on it. Just yards before this is a delight-ful waterfall under a flowery bank.

This is the start of the highlight, the Ashgill Force loop. Don't cross the bridge, but take the path continuing up the bank to a kiss-ing-gate into its increasingly tighter environs. The clear path runs into its wooded ravine, soon revealing a series of low but smashing waterfalls on it, further enhanced on my visit by the presence of a dipper perched on a streamside boulder. Approaching the upper fall, the real Ashgill Force appears ahead, somewhat bizarrely directly beneath a very high stone arched road bridge.

17

Waterfall below Ashgill Force

Cross a footbridge to enter a splendid amphitheatre. *Alongside are remains from lead mining of Ashgill Horse Level, three stone bays that were 'bouse-teams' for the storing of lead ore: the minor spoil heaps and surrounds are well decorated by flowers. The fall itself tumbles over a big craggy rim, much like Hardraw Force in Wensleydale.* Advance on the path towards the base of the fall, ascending then running beneath the scar. *Standard practice is to continue until you are literally behind the waterfall (with care underfoot), this sizeable overhang being quite the driest place to be if you should be hit by a sudden shower!*

Retrace steps to the clearing, but instead of re-crossing the bridge, take an inviting grassy miners' way slanting up to the left, well below the end of the cliff. This runs to a gate/stile on the edge of the gill. Pass through and along the fenceside to the lone house at Bird's Nest. In front, bear right down its side to a gate below. Now a good grassy path descends the fieldside, with super views over the dale and down into the lower gill. At the bottom it drops steeply to the footbridge on the cross-paths.

Cross the bridge on Ash Gill and head away through an old wall, ascending a steep, grassy track up the bank. Along the top it runs to the buildings at Ashgillside. Take a stile on the right and up the outside of the house to a stile just past it. Now cross over the drive, using several stiles in succession as you reach a parallel drive to the cluster of houses in front, with Ashgillside House on the left. Head on between them, turning left round the back to a farmyard.

Note the 1734 dated lintel on the left, then take a stile on the right alongside a barn. Back in the fields, head away to a stile at the end. *Now you can savour big views to rolling moorland beyond the pastures across the valley.* Maintain this dead-level course through several fields. Watch for a stile just below a barn at the end, then pass along a field-top beneath a short row of cottages (Pasture Houses) to a corner-stile onto the terminus of a surfaced lane. Cross straight over and along a short drive to farm buildings ahead. Entering the yard, pass through a gate on the left and slant down to the far corner of the field, with Garrigill just below. Pass through a wall-stile with steps behind, then down across a tiny wooded gill and along to follow the top of a wooded bank above the river, emerging at the end by cottages at a charming corner. Turn left over Garrigill Bridge and you're back in the village centre.

Garrigill, South Tynedale, as seen from the Corpse Road

4

AROUND NENTHEAD

START *Nenthead*   *Grid ref.* NY 781436

DISTANCE *5¹2 miles (9km)*

ORDNANCE SURVEY MAPS
1:50,000
Landranger 86 - Haltwhistle & Brampton or
Landranger 87 - Hexham & Haltwhistle
1:25,000
Explorer OL31 - North Pennines (Teesdale/Weardale)

ACCESS *Start from the village centre. Car park. Served by bus from Alston (some start from Carlisle).*

A low level walk through pastures at the head of the Nent Valley, surrounded by rich remains of the lead mining industry

Nenthead is an archetypal North Pennine lead mining village at the head of the valley of the River Nent, which flows to meet the South Tyne in Alston. An altitude of over 1400ft earns its claim to be England's highest village, a point that the smaller Flash, in Staffordshire, would dispute at more than 1500ft. Nestling in a bowl of high and lonely moorland, Nenthead is home to Nenthead Mines Heritage Centre operated by the North Pennines Heritage Trust on the site of a smelt mill. In addition to a trail around the mining area, it has underground tours, cafe and giftshop.

Nenthead was laid out as a model village by the influential London Lead Company, who ran the mining operations of Alston Moor during the industry's heyday, along with those over the watershed in Teesdale. The company's founders were enthusiastic members of the Society of Friends, leading to them being better known as the 'Quaker Company'. A philanthropic approach provided *their employees and families with facilities that would put better heeled communities to shame. Many aspects of social and cultural life were catered for: Nenthead folk had a school and a library that were impressive indeed for the early 19th century, while the old Lead Company Workmens Reading Rooms are still evident in the village centre. Around this time Nenthead's population peaked at something like 2000. The company encouraged workers to make the most of their time above ground by providing space around their cottages for allotments, and encouraged them to maintain smallholdings from the rough enclosures surrounding the village.*

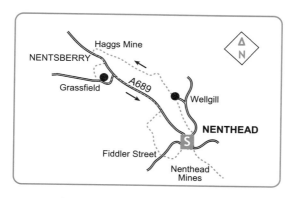

Despite the company's desire to see their workforce pursue sober interests, the village still supported several pubs of which, appropriately enough, the Miners Arms survives. There is also a Post office/shop and the Overwater Restaurant (until recently the Crown Inn). Also prominent in the centre is a cast-iron fountain, this being a twin of one in Middleton-in-Teesdale dedicated to the company's agent Robert Bainbridge. Next to the shop stands a large Wesleyan Church of 1873. John Wesley first preached at Nenthead in 1748, and the Methodist movement became stronger as the London Lead Company pulled out towards the end of the 19th century. While the last true lead mine closed in 1919, mineral extraction projects continued decades longer. A Belgian company re-worked old spoilheaps for zinc, while fluorspar and even silver *were commercially obtained. Though the mining heyday had passed many decades earlier, only in recent times have there been major efforts at environmental improvements. Whatever happens on the surface, however, an unseen legacy is no less than forty miles of underground tunnels! One business that began in mining days and survives into the 21st century is that of Wright Brothers: originating with a horse and cart in 1914, today their buses still carry passengers across the moors and dales of the Alston area.*

From the junction by the fountain, take the road signed to Greenends, and within seconds fork left up a cobbled street. Becoming surfaced at the top, a sharp bend right is reached. Here go straight ahead on a rough road, past the old school to end at a house. Keep on through a small enclosure and then on a walled way that passes above the modest church of St John the Evangelist. The way then starts to slant up to the right. Don't follow it but take a stile in the wall ahead to emerge into a sloping meadow. *In season this supports a rampant display of purple orchids, while very evident down below is a large reclaimed mining site.* Follow the field bottom to the end, and from a corner stile cross to a house. A gate leads onto its short drive, out past the house onto a lane at Wellgill.

Go left a few yards, over the bridge, then at another drive take a stile directly in front. Rise past the house along its lawn to a stile out into a field. Bear gently left to the far end, and from a stile/gate bear right across an old mining site to a stile just short of Gudham Gill. Slant left down to a footbridge on this stream flowing over a slabby bed. Go left a couple of steps on the track across it, then take a stile by the wall corner on the right, ascending the wallside towards a house. Partway up, take a stile in the wall and cross to a fence on the left. Don't pass through but turn right with it, through an intervening stile below the house and on to the corner. Here a stile sends you down to an adjacent one into the top of a plantation, a long established woodland that does not appear on the map! Turn right along its top side, easier progress being a few trees down, to reach a stile at the end. Continue along a field top, taking a gate in the adjacent wall just short of the end. *These fields' occupants might surprise you, for this is home to a herd of llamas. That's right, llamas, thousands of miles from their natural home in South America!*

Resume on the other side to a corner stile beneath a belt of trees, and then straight along the field bottoms, a fine level march through good sheep pastures passing through a stand of trees at the end. *Wide views over the valley look to rough moorland slopes above isolated farms.* Emerging from the stile into a field, go straight across to a stile in the facing wall. Joining a rough track at Haggs Bank, turn down it, continuing down a drive onto the main road at Nentsberry. *Immediately on your left is the dark entrance to a sizeable adit: built to drain the mineshafts it still emits an appreciable quantity of water. An old building alongside has a Victorian postbox affixed. The various remains hereabouts are all part of the former Haggs Mine, which closed in the 1930s. Just along the road is a caravan park at the former Horse & Waggon pub, and there is a former Wesleyan Chapel of 1825 just beyond.* Go left just as far as Nentsberry Bridge high above the river, then double back right on the drive to a pair of cottages. Turn sharp left in front of Clog Hall, up to a stile into a field. An inviting path ascends above a flowery stream and past grassy spoil heaps. At the top take a gate on the left and out past the house onto a back road. Turn left, ascending past a farm (Grassfield) then curving round to rejoin the main road.

Turn right for a long half-mile on the wide road, perhaps making use of its grass verges: a pavement appears as the Nenthead sign is passed. Dropping down towards the edge of the village, turn right alongside Kings Head Cottages where a driveway bears off to the right. This steeply ascends a fieldside to Donks Hall. Don't turn along the drive to the house, but take a stile just above and ascend to the wall above (not quite as the map suggests). Don't pass through but go left alongside the wall, passing high above the house and on to a wall-stile at the end. You are now looking down onto Nenthead. Slant up the reedy field, a faint grassy track over a cross-paths (again not as per map) to a gateway in an old wall above. Here a firmer track runs left along the wallside to a gate. Simply remain on this level track past several old barns at Fiddler Street and along to a gate onto a steep road.

Turn a few paces to the right and take a stile on the left. *The stand of tall conifers opposite was planted largely to provide timber for use in the mines.* A thin path doubles back down the wallside to a stile into Dowgang Hush. *A 'hush' was a deep channel in the hillside caused by the release of water that had previously been dammed higher up. The result was the tearing away of loose material to hopefully reveal a promising vein of ore.* Turn left on a path descending by the Dowgang Burn. Through a stile at the bottom a grassy track passes through to the edge of the village at Overwater, amid the largely whitewashed houses at Dene Terrace. For a direct finish, turn right on the road to the centre, just ahead.

To link to the Nenthead Mines area, bear right between these cottages to find a broad path running upstream to a footbridge over the stream, with the splendid big stone-arched entrance of the Dowgang Level just upstream. Over the footbridge cross to Nenthead Mines, with the visitor centre just ahead. Even if not patronising the hugely absorbing visitor centre, then the walk should still be completed with a cursory exploration of its environs.

Turn right on the stony track past the main building, and you will encounter many splendid features of this remarkable outdoor museum including a new waterwheel complex. At Mill Cottage pass through the gate and ascend the stony track amid a remarkable mining legacy, featuring spoil heaps, reservoirs, water-cuts, levels and adits. *Note that while you are upon a right of way here, some features such as restored buildings are part of the visitor centre tour.* As the track levels out, just a few paces up to your left is the Handsome Mea Reservoir, which perhaps makes a convenient turning point. *Evident at the side is a stone-lined leat serving it, one of a network of such channels carrying water around the site. This sizeable sheet of water powered, among other things, a huge waterwheel.* Retrace steps to the visitor centre and back to the village.

The fountain, Nenthead

NENT VALLEY

START *Alston*   *Grid ref. NY 718464*

DISTANCE *8¹⁄4 miles (13km)*

ORDNANCE SURVEY MAPS
1:50,000
Landranger 86 - Haltwhistle & Brampton **or**
Landranger 87 - Hexham & Haltwhistle
1:25,000
Explorer OL31 - North Pennines (Teesdale/Weardale)

ACCESS *Start from the market cross halfway up the main street. Car parking nearby, also a car park at the station. Served by bus from Haltwhistle, Carlisle, Hexham and Penrith.*

> *A super exploration of the side valley of the Nent upstream from Alston, linking riverside walking, lead mining sites, old hamlets and great views from colourful meadows*

For more on Alston, see page 9. From the Market Cross turn down the setted side road dropping away at the rear, into a square where turn right to the Gossipgate Gallery. Continuing, the town is left behind and the lane becomes briefly surfaced before dropping stonily down between walls to reach the bank of the River Nent. *Immediately across the river is the site of an old quarry. The colour of the stream is a long-surviving legacy of lead mining days.* Follow the Nent upstream to where the track bridges it, with Gossipgate Cottage just across and an appealing low waterfall immediately upstream. Don't cross the bridge (it will be crossed at the end of the walk) but take a stile to advance upstream on the grassy bank. Beyond another stile the path enters a short-lived wooded bank, then resumes alongside the Nent.

The path remains by the river, other than at one short section where a tiny plank bridge leads to a stile, only to quickly return to the Nent side of the fence. Further, another short section of woodland is entered, soon emerging at a delightful spot on the grassy bank, alongside a lovely little waterfall into a deep circular green pool. Just ahead, the path ascends a minor bank to a stile, then back to the riverbank again for a level, more open stroll alongside it to arrive at a road at Blagill Bridge. Turn left over the concrete bridge, and follow the lane uphill alongside the little stream of Blagill Burn to enter the farming hamlet of Blagill. *As the walk will return to this point, you have the option of a much more modest 3½-mile circuit by omitting the Nenthall loop.*

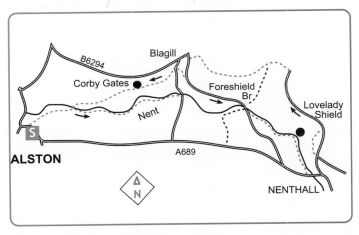

A few steps beyond the phone box, bear right along a rough access road between houses. At the last one the track swings steeply right down to cross a stone arched bridge over Blagill Burn. Heading away, immediately halt to look down on a delectable cascade over a rocky lip. The enclosed track then slants up onto the B6294, turn right. *This section enjoys splendid views over the Nent Valley, with the river flowing through an old mining site on the broad flats below.* Remain on this quiet road as it curves around to slant all the way down to Foreshield Bridge, a fine two-arched structure on the

Nent. *Note that the rough road to the left offers another short-cut, through West Foreshield and up to the return route.*

Across the bridge take a stile on the left and head upstream, a lovely walk with the farm and cottage opposite at West Foreshield. Partway on, a stile in the adjacent fence sends the path across a couple of meadows to short-cut a bend of the river, though most users tend to remain with the bank. Rejoining at another stile, cross a sidestream and resume by the bank, passing into trees at the end to emerge onto a driveway alongside the stone-arched bridge to Lovelady Shield, currently operating as a hotel.

Cross the access road, not the bridge, and continue upstream through park-like surrounds. *The way passes a deep, stone-lined circular shaft, reassuringly firmly covered. This was an air vent for the Nent Force mine level: this major feat of engineering was effectively an underground canal used to drain various levels, and extended for more than four miles. Its designer was John Smeaton, better known for the Eddystone Lighthouse.* As Nenthall Bridge appears ahead, a stile in the adjacent fence sends you to the other side of the wall to run on through a gate and a couple of stiles to emerge onto the A689 opposite the hotel. *Nent Hall was built early in the 18th century on the profits of a successful strike of lead ore on the slopes above. Nent Hall is currently a country house hotel serving bar meals, a potentially well placed midway point.*

This is indeed the walk's turning point, so go left over the bridge to the junction at the war memorial. *This records the loss of no less than six men from this rural backwater during the First World War.* Turn left again along the side road which climbs steeply then reaches a fork. The simplest option takes the minor road straight ahead, though there is greater interest in taking a stile on the left to descend by a sunken way to the field bottom, with a footbridge on a sidestream just ahead. Pass to the right of the photogenic ruin of High Lovelady Shield. *This was a bastle dating back some 400 years, incorporating an older defensive pele tower. In times of Border unrest the owner would move his livestock into the ground floor of this fortified farmhouse and his family onto the upper floor.* From here take the grassy old track ascending to the right, above a wall. Partway up, cut off with another sunken way ascending more steeply, then up and across the field to a stile/gate back onto the minor road.

Go left on this no through road. *Extensive views look over the Nent Valley's meadows and down to the South Tyne valley, with the Pennine watershed beyond the top of Alston from this the walk's high point of about 1410ft/430m.* After a generally level course the road finally expires at a fork, where two stony tracks head off. While that to the right heads for the moors, take the one descending left, a wide walled cart track on past a small plantation. Ignore a branch down to the left, which is the short-cut climbing from West Foreshield. The track now runs a grand course along the hillside, passing beneath a line of largely grassed over spoil heaps from a once busy lead mining location.

Rising steadily the track reaches a gate on the brow, with the side valley of Blagill in front. *Further ahead is the higher part of Alston, with Grey Nag and neighbouring fells behind: the summit of Cross Fell also appears over to the left, its northern scarp prominent before undulating along to Melmerby Fell. Just over to the right is the extremely isolated house at Blagillhead.* Largely surfaced now, the way winds down past Clinty Brow Farm and more old workings back onto the B6294.

Foreshield Bridge, River Nent

Go right to cross Blagill Bridge, and a little further fork left down the road back into Blagill. Just above the phone box turn right before a barn on a bridleway signed to Alston. Pass through the farmyard to a gate into a field, and a grassy way heads off alongside a wall. This runs along two further fieldsides to Corby Gates Farm, enjoying big views over the Nent Valley. A pair of bridle-gates point along the fieldtop in front of the buildings, to a gate onto an enclosed track. Go left on this away from Corby Gates to a gate into a field overlooking a steeper drop to the river.

The top of this bank affords an excellent view update to the Nenthead area, and also looks down on the outward route, with the Cross Fell skyline on the southern horizon. Turn right on an inviting fieldside track. Shortly after a gate this turns to slant down the field alongside a fence. Passing through a gate in it resume down the other side, through a gate and down open pasture to a pair of gates at the bottom. From a stile by the lower one, a delightful leafy footway runs an enclosed course to soon emerge above Gossipgate Cottage. Dropping to merge with its grassy drive, this leads back out to the bridge. Cross it to finish the walk as it began along Gossipgate into the centre of Alston.

River Nent at Gossipgate Cottage

SOUTH TYNE VIEWS

START *Alston*   Grid ref. *NY 718464*

DISTANCE *4¹₂ miles (7km)*

ORDNANCE SURVEY MAPS
1:50,000
Landranger 86 - Haltwhistle & Brampton **or**
Landranger 87 - Hexham & Haltwhistle
1:25,000
Explorer OL31 - North Pennines (Teesdale / Weardale)

ACCESS *Start from the market cross halfway up the main street. Car parking nearby, also a car park at the station. Served by bus from Haltwhistle, Carlisle, Hexham and Penrith.*

> *A leisurely, relaxing stroll by the river south of Alston, returning at a slightly higher level to enjoy wider views*

For more on Alston, see page 9. Descend the main street to the T-junction (note the old milestone set into the wall), then go left along the Penrith road until approaching the bridge on the river. Take a stile in the wall on the left and a path drops to the river-bank to head upstream through woodland. After a short spell on the stone slabbed bank, the path forks. Bear off left here, rising a little to meet another path in front of a wall. Turn right on this fine path above the wooded bank. Bridging a tiny stream at the end a stile takes you out to continue in a meadow, still with a wall on the left. From a stile at the end you're back on top of a little bank. The path runs a very straight line, as the next stile transfers you over the wall and along the field bottoms. Entering a large field beyond a small field bottom, towards the end angle across to a stile and footbridge on a lively sidestream.

Back out, this time an inviting grassy way crosses two fields to pass beneath the old farm at Low Nest. *Ahead now are big open views to the Cross Fell skyline, with Melmerby Fell alongside.* Keep on through a gateway beneath the farm, then two wall-stiles, then on with a crumbling wall past a stand of trees. From the next wall-stile you're back on the field tops, almost, passing by the white walled house at Low Cowgap to a gateway/stile in the wall ahead. Advance through a field centre, and on through a gateway. The farm at Bleagate appears ahead and a wall on the left leads to it. Pass to the right of the first barn, then left into the farmyard. Rise straight up to the access road, which is immediately surfaced.

This is the walk's turning point. Though you could follow the road away, a footpath option is nicer. Go immediately left through a gateway and slant up the small enclosure to a stile into an equally small plantation. Quickly emerging from trees, bear left across the field to re-enter the belt of trees further on. Pass through to the wall behind to find a stile there. Cross the field towards the house at Woodstock at the far end. From a gate in front, an overgrown grassy track rises to rejoin the road in front of the house.

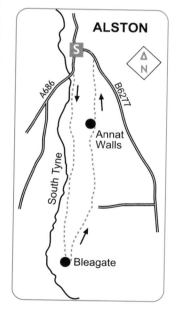

Turn left along this access road as far as a sharp bend right. Here go left, briefly, along High Nest's stony driveway, but leave quite early by a wall-stile on the right. Cross the field to a stile at the end, and on again on the top edge of a lawn-like meadow to a deep wooded side gill, Nattrass Gill. The path drops to a footbridge in the trees, then round to a bigger one on the main stream, with a lovely waterfall literally underneath.

Swing back out of the trees to resume along a field bottom, continuing on to approach the farm buildings at Annat Walls. Go straight on to the corner gate, and head on past the various buildings. Continue on out past some barns (noting a 1707 datestone above a door) on the access road. This runs on with wide views over the dale, passing another farm and approaching the top end of Alston. With modern suburbia in front, go through a kissing-gate and follow the suburban street along to the top end of the main street. Descend the street to finish, noting in particular the Friends' Meeting House, a lovely old building on your left.

Alston

THE WARDWAY

START Alston   *Grid ref.* NY 718464

DISTANCE 6 miles (9½km)

ORDNANCE SURVEY MAPS
1:50,000
Landranger 86 - Haltwhistle & Brampton *or*
Landranger 87 - Hexham & Haltwhistle
1:25,000
Explorer OL31 - North Pennines (Teesdale/Weardale)

ACCESS Start from the market cross halfway up the main street.
Car parking nearby, also a car park at the station. Served by bus
from Haltwhistle, Carlisle, Hexham and Penrith.

> *A gentle valley walk to Leadgate is followed by a higher
> level parallel march along the old track of the Wardway,
> with correspondingly wide views over the Alston area*

For more on Alston, see page 9. Descend the main street to the
T-junction (note the milestone set into the wall), then go left along
the Penrith road to the bridge on the South Tyne. Immediately
across turn down to the left on a splendid enclosed path tracing the
South Tyne upstream. *Further updale the plateau top of Cross Fell
forms a lofty skyline.* Quickly passed is a substantial ruin. After a
grand section the path enters scrub, and is forced through a fence
gap into the adjacent field. The river flows particularly wide and
stony around this point. Resume along here to rise to a stile into
trees at the end. The path then runs atop the wooded bank to
reach a small sidestream at the end. Here take a stile on the right
and head directly away from the river: as the adjacent tiny stream
disappears, a wall leads along to a stile onto the Leadgate Road.

Turn left past the house at Crosslands, and just a little further to Scale Bank farm drive also on the left. Pass through the gate but then immediately branch off the drive to cross to the far corner of the field, the onset of a very pleasant crossing of sheep pastures. From a stile in the corner cross an often-dry rocky bedded stream to a stile opposite. *Limestone walls add character to the mini-ravine where the stream may have sprung to life just to your left.*

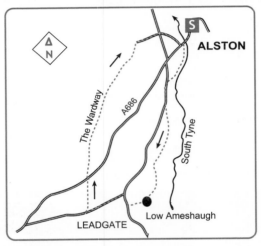

From the stile head directly away on a faint groove, but before the minor brow bear right to a wall-stile. Cross a longer, sloping field to a stile at the far end, just above the corner. Follow the wall to the far end, and from the stile cross the large flat field to the left-most of two gates visible, further left than the farm at Low Ameshaugh. From this gate bear right towards the farm, and take the first gate to cross a small enclosure to a gate into the farmyard. Go straight ahead on the drive leading out, and this runs between walls, becoming surfaced to rise onto the road in Leadgate.

Turn right up past the few houses, just as far as a T-junction on the brow. *This is watched over by an old roadsign still bearing the legend 'Cumberland County Council', along with a phone box.* Turn left up the Penrith road, starting with a punishingly steep haul out of the hamlet. The gradients ease in stages, revealing more of the Cross Fell massif and the upper dale as height is gained. After a good half-mile the road actually levels out, very briefly, and this is the point to leave, alongside a small electricity station. Turn right up a walled track, leveling out at once to commence the long return along the old road of the Wardway. This firm surfaced lane runs between walls and recently planted trees to quickly reach the A686. *Alongside is one of a series of old milestones that punctuate the main road's long run over Hartside.*

Cross straight over and resume as before, remaining on this track all the way to the end. A level section precedes crossing the moorland stream of Gill Burn to rise to the brow. *At 1342ft/409m this is the walk's high point, and a welcome seat awaits. Relax and enjoy wide views over South Tynedale, with Alston an irrepressible magnet. Alongside, an occupation track rises between wide verges onto the moor.* The way now commences a prolonged, steady descent, passing further seats before finally reaching a sharp bend. Here it becomes surfaced and drops to the right to emerge past housing onto the A689 Brampton road at a crossroads. Cross and bear right on the main road, dropping down to meet the A686 again alongside Alston's war memorial. Go left over the bridge to finish.

A corner of Alston

WHITLEY CASTLE

8

START *Alston*   *Grid ref. NY 718464*

DISTANCE *6³4 miles (11km)*

ORDNANCE SURVEY MAPS
1:50,000
Landranger 86 - Haltwhistle & Brampton **or**
Landranger 87 - Hexham & Haltwhistle
1:25,000
Explorer OL31 - North Pennines (Teesdale/Weardale)

ACCESS *Start from the market cross halfway up the main street. Car parking nearby, also a car park at the station. Served by bus from Haltwhistle, Carlisle, Hexham and Penrith.*

A low level stroll in the South Tyne Valley, linking the Pennine Way and South Tyne Trails to visit a charismatic Roman fort

For a note on Alston, see page 9. Descend the main street to the T-junction (note the old milestone), then go left along the Penrith road to the bridge on the South Tyne. Cross and advance to the A689 Brampton junction alongside Alston's war memorial. Turn right and within a few yards bear right along a drive. This is shared with the Pennine Way, as is the entire outward route to Kirkhaugh. Keep left on this drive, past the houses, along to a field whose top leads towards a lone house. A small gate to its left sends an enclosed path on past its grounds. *This neighbourhood gives views of the town back across the river.* Continue to the far end where a stile admits into a field. A faint path heads away outside a wood to a kissing-gate at the very end, just across a farm track. Resume through a gateway and on to imposing gates at the end. Through the small gate a stream is bridged to be faced with the impressive house at Harbut Lodge. Bear left up the hedgeside, going left through a gate between outbuildings and along past another house. Swing right along its far side and, ignoring the drive to the right, remain on the fieldside. Curve around its corner and partway along is a stile onto the parallel drive. Go left up this back onto the A689.

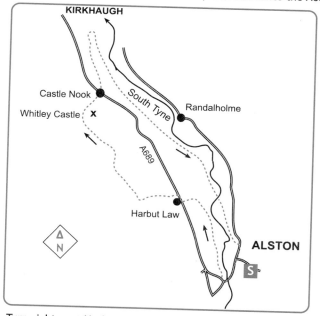

Turn right past Harbut Law and take a kissing-gate on the left. A track rises towards the farm buildings, but bear slightly right off it to a gate in front (right of all buildings). Across a trickle a thin path ascends the field with a wall on the left. *A grand view opens out, with Alston still on show beneath a big moorland skyline.* A little moist, things improves after crossing a small stream. Towards the top swing right to short-cut the corner, crossing instead to the right-hand corner. Ignore the enclosed way rising away from a gate, and take a wall-stile on the right. Here begins a splendid section on a broad path heading directly away down the pasture. The route remains dead straight through several pastures punctuated by stiles to ultimately arrive above the deep trough of the Gilderdale Burn. *Ahead during this stage is a sweeping prospect of Whitley Common rising to the 2152ft/656m summit of Grey Nag across Gilderdale, as well as a longer view down the main valley.*

At the bottom the path slants down to a footbridge on the peaty burn. *This delightful stream forms the county boundary, as Cumberland (now Cumbria) gives way to Northumberland: the opposite bank makes an excellent spot to break journey.* Across, the path slants right up the bank, close by the wall. Soon easing out and fading, cross to a ladder-stile in the wall ahead. Now ascend a better pasture with a fence on your left, leveling out to join a farm track rising from Whitlow down to the right. Bear left up this to a gate/stile in the wall above.

The track fades but the route is clear, crossing the pasture to a gate in the fence ahead. Immediately on your right now is the Roman fort of Whitley Castle. *Increasingly evident are its grassy ramparts encircling a central platform, highly distinctive and quite stirring. Note how farmers paid no heed to this ancient monument as they built their walls through the heart of the site. Unique as the only Roman fort within the North Pennines, it stands by their road known as the Maiden Way, which linked Kirkby Thore in the Eden Valley to Carvoran near Greenhead, in the shadow of Hadrian's Wall. This is explored more fully in WALK 10.*

Through the gate the clearer track curves right as it contours the slope, dropping nearer the wall enclosing the fort. It becomes firmer and joins the wall to pass through a gate/stile in it, with the fort very impressive just in front. Drop directly left to the farm at Castle Nook. A fence-stile on the left avoids the farm, sending a path down to cross the parallel stream and descend the plantation edge to emerge back onto the main road. Cross to the phone box and take the adjacent gate, then bear left along the field top. You are now on the line of the Maiden Way Roman road. Through a gate at the end the way has been diverted away from the cottages at Dyke House. *The Romans would have taken less kindly to house-building astride their road!* Cross the paddock to a stile on the right, then pass outside the enclosing wall to rejoin the true line at the gate at the end of the field. Just ahead is a stone arched bridge which marks the turning point of the walk. *Alongside the wall, meanwhile, underfoot, is a very distinct shallow trough, surely of the Romans' making?* Pass through another gate then at the field-end, leave both the Pennine Way and Maiden Way by turning right to that sturdy bridge on the railway line terminus at Kirkhaugh.

Kirkhaugh is no more than a hamlet just to the north of here, though the station it lost in the 1970s has been returned to it, if only as a tourist amenity. Across the bridge turn right to a stile accessing the South Tyne Trail at Kirkhaugh Station, which from here to Alston has been usurped by the restored narrow-gauge line. *When trains are operating, refreshments are normally available from an old guard's van: the platform can be accessed through a little gate before crossing the bridge. The extension from Gilderdale to Kirkhaugh was opened in 1999. Intriguingly, it can only be accessed by either train or footpath.*

So the simple return is along the South Tyne Trail, shared with the railway for almost three miles back to Alston. To alleviate safety fears, path and railway are separated by a fence. *After an early viaduct there are varied views over the river below, across which stands Kirkhaugh's church of the Holy Paraclete. Completed in 1869, it is notable for a remarkable, needle-thin spire.* The county boundary is re-crossed on the impressive Gilderdale Viaduct, high above the tumbling burn. *Note the commemorative boundary signs affixed.* Across, a wooden platform survives from the preserved line's previous terminus, Gilderdale Halt. Continuing, there are some good open views and spells in the river's company: *there is also a glimpse back to Randalholme, downstream across the river, with its origins as a 14th century defensive pele tower.*

Passing beneath a massive stone bridge and a bend into a cutting, Alston's church spire points skyward directly above, with even a glimpse of Cross Fell's summit beyond. The river's welcome company is cemented as the railway crosses it in a particularly nice setting. The path crosses the line before the first large sheds heralding the fringe of Alston station, remaining on this side all the way to the terminus. *Just short of the end, the confluence of the South Tyne and Nent is witnessed.* The home of England's highest narrow-gauge railway, Alston station has a signal box, gift shop, refreshments, an exhibition of transport memorabilia and a model railway centre in the old goods yard. Trains run at most holiday periods, and virtually daily in July and August.

9

KNARSDALE

START *Slaggyford*   *Grid ref.* **NY 680519**

DISTANCE *6½ miles (10½km)*

ORDNANCE SURVEY MAPS
1:50,000
Landranger 86 - Haltwhistle & Brampton
1:25,000
Explorer OL43 - Hadrian's Wall

ACCESS *Start from a roadside parking area at the Barhaugh Hall junction at Thompson's Well Bridge, on the A689 a quarter-mile south of the village. Served by Carlisle/Brampton-Alston buses.*

The peaceful communities of mid-South Tynedale form a focus for this walk combining a fine section of the Pennine Way with a valley side return offering super views from an equally super path

Begin by following the road north into the centre of Slaggyford, with a caravan site on your right. Turn left at the first chance up a side road ascending the green. *Slaggyford is a sleepy community between the South Tyne river to the east and the South Tyne Trail which traces the old railway to the west. Its spacious green is the focal point, while just above it the old station buildings survive in an evocative setting. For a simpler walk to Knarsdale, continue up to the old station and follow the Trail all the way to Burnstones: you cross both Knarsdale and Burnstones viaducts before joining the road to double back past Burnstones to pass under the viaduct then on a back road to Knarsdale churchyard.*

The road rises from the top of the green towards the station, but before that turn right on the Pennine Way in front of a former chapel. The track quickly becomes a splendid grassy pathway to meet a cart track coming off the adjacent old rail line. Turn right along the track, rising above the line and past an arched bridge over it, where the track ends. Remain on the continuing path, enclosed by a wall from the fields on the right. It drops gently into trees, crossing a tiny footbridge and running pleasantly down to a more substantial footbridge on the Knar Burn, in a splendid setting in the shadow of the tall arches of Knarsdale Viaduct. Across the bridge turn downstream a few yards then go left to a gate out into a field beneath the line. Advance with the wall over a small, channelled watercourse, then turn left to pass through a railway underpass.

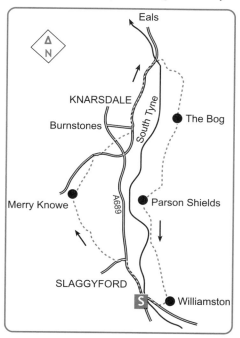

At the other side a sunken grassy track rises up the fieldside, swinging right at the end and rising to pass through a gateway. It continues up the field and crosses to the farm at Merry Knowe.

Enter the yard by a gate, turn right along the fenceside to find a wall-stile at the end. A little enclosed path runs on to the rear of the cottages, across a yard, a further stile and a lawn to a facing wall-stile at the end. Back in the fields, head directly away from the house just as far as a rickety gate guarding a stile in the wall on the left. Head off down the centre of this broad spur, on through a ladder-stile then a wall-stile and down a bank to a simple foot-bridge and across to a gate onto a back road.

Turn right, bridging the South Tyne Trail and on a little further to a gate on the left. Head away, bearing right across the field to a gateway and wall junction where a stile is cleverly hidden in the corner. Head across the field centre to locate a wall-stile onto the A689. Cross straight over to another and along the wallside to a stile into Knarsdale churchyard. *St Jude's church was erected in 1838 and restored in 1892, and features a bell-cote. The list of rectors notes that Thomas Todhunter, early 19th century incumbent, froze to death in a field near Williamston (encountered near the end of this walk).* A stile leads onto the road at the front, to find the welcoming Kirkstyle Inn alongside. *Originally named the Church Stile & Sportsmans Rest, it is an ideal place to break journey.*

Turn left on the road and keep straight on at the junction by the churchyard wall, passing Knarsdale Hall on the right. *This solid farmhouse dates from the 17th century.* Bridging the Thinhope Burn this back lane runs pleasantly along to Eals Bridge. *This is a fine crossing of the South Tyne, a graceful two-arched structure with good views of some splendid river scenery. Upstream, note the farm at The Bog perched on the hillside directly above.* Across the bridge turn immediately upstream on a rough road through woodland. This quickly leaves the river and swings left to rise to a fork. Keep right on the main way, crossing a wooden bridge on inflowing Snope Burn. It then winds steeply up the other side, high above the wooded edge before turning right to run a contrastingly level course along the fieldsides to its terminus at The Bog, an idyllically sited and isolated farmstead.

Pass through the cobbled yard, bearing left at the end to a gate across a concrete yard. Advance to another gate just across the small enclosure, and a grand track heads away across the base of the fell. Initially with a wall for company it runs beneath a steep heathery bank under Snope Common, part of the massive tract of

Whitfield Moor. After a gate the wall drops away and a still better open section commences: savour the finest promenade imaginable on a delectable greensward across colourful slopes. *Sweeping views embrace South Tynedale, featuring Knarsdale, Burnstones and its viaduct, the river splashing through wide stony flats, and fields giving way to a magnificent moorland backdrop pierced by the Knar Burn and the smaller Thinhope Burn. Steep slopes above the path show evidence of abandoned lead workings.*

Towards the end the way forks: take the main branch slanting down to the right. It immediately passes a well preserved limekiln. The track drops more steeply to a gate off the fell, and advances above modern barns to the farmhouse at Parson Shields. Through the gate in front, turn immediately left on a grassy track climbing steeply away. This eases and fades as it runs to a gateway in the wall ahead. Pass through the gate and follow the left side of the fence across a broad pasture. A gate at the end sends a path on through attractive mixed woodland.

Emerging at the other side an inviting grassy track heads away, approaching a wood and rising gently left above it. Towards the end a track comes in from the left and leads to a gate ahead. Below is the farm at Williamston, and the track drops down the rough bank to a gate in front. Cross to the yard, noting the 1657 datestone incorporated into the house wall. Turn right on the farm road out to join a back road. Go right, enjoying another brief spell with the South Tyne to Thompson's Well Bridge. *On this side, downstream, a stile gives access to Williamston nature reserve of the Northumberland Wildlife Trust.* The South Tyne is re-crossed to rejoin the A689 to finish.

St Jude's church, Knarsdale

43

10

THE MAIDEN WAY

START Lambley   Grid ref. NY 671584

DISTANCE 7 miles (11km)

ORDNANCE SURVEY MAPS
1:50,000
Landranger 86 - Haltwhistle & Brampton
1:25,000
Explorer OL43 - Hadrian's Wall

ACCESS Start from the A689 at the top of the village, there is a good sized parking area on the top side of the road by the bend where the cul-de-sac Lambley road drops away. Served by Carlisle/Brampton-Alston buses and also from Haltwhistle.

> *Two distinctly different yet parallel routes on the western side of the South Tyne Valley, out on an old rail line, returning on the course of a Roman road*

Lambley is a tiny village huddled away from the main road on a steep slope above the South Tyne, known for its railway viaduct on the old Haltwhistle-Alston line. Previously Harper Town, the name Lambley comes from a farm near the river. A convent of Benedictine nuns here was supposedly sacked by Scottish liberator William Wallace ('Braveheart') during a particularly bloodthirsty foray in the late 13th century. At one time Lambley was even a railway junction, with the enterprising Brampton & Hartleyburn Railway branching west to serve collieries between here and Brampton. Indeed, for just a short time it connected Alston to the outside world prior to completion of the viaduct.

From the former chapel at the junction, descend the road towards Lambley centre but turn off almost at once at a gate on the right. An access track drops away, and at the bottom go straight on through a small gate. From here a partly grassed over tarmac path descends the fieldside, steeply at the bottom to enter the woods below. Emerging onto a path junction, continue straight down to find yourself crossing an old railway. *This is not the 'main' Haltwhistle-Alston branch, but the aforementioned mineral railway.* Dropping straight down the other side the mighty pillars of Lambley Viaduct suddenly appear straight in front. The path slants right, down wooden steps to a crossroads in the wood. *For the pleasure of standing on the viaduct and admiring the view, take a short detour right to ascend iron steps onto it to savour this spectacular setting! The viaduct is crossed during the course of WALK 11, which describes it further.*

Unfortunately this end of the viaduct is an impasse, as the way is barred by private grounds at Lambley's old station. Back at the path crossroads the continuing route crosses straight over and down again, passing under a side arch of the viaduct. By the lowest point you are almost at river level. The path however immediately turns to re-ascend, wooden steps climbing to run beneath the restored, now private station house at Lambley. Running beneath the old buildings the line is rejoined, and shared by the driveway. *At this point look back to enjoy a fine prospect of the viaduct.* Advance on to soon reach a junction with an access road alongside a cottage. Cross straight over to a gate

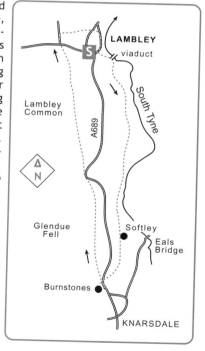

accessing the line's continuation, now as a friendlier track. *This provides a splendid stride with fine views over the valley while keeping an eye out for some interesting lineside carvings.*

After crossing the drive to Whitwham Farm the track approaches Glendue Wood enclosing Glendue Burn. This is crossed by the impressive Glendue Viaduct, a tall five-arched structure. Forging on, much of this next stage is through the varied foliage of Softley Low Wood. You emerge at the approach to Softley Farm, whose access road crosses a high stone-arched bridge over the line. *Woodland is now replaced by contrastingly open and magnificent views across the river to a tangle of farmland rising to a long moorland skyline.* Gradually the valley road comes in from the right, and at an informal parking area and access point, switch to the road to resume for the two minutes to Burnstones. Here the long, low viaduct across the Thinhope Burn emphatically marks the turning point of the walk, as the South Tyne Trail is traded for the Pennine Way. *First, however, consider a short detour to Knarsdale, where church and pub stand shoulder to shoulder (see WALK 9). Simply pass under the viaduct and go left along the side road.*

Without passing under the viaduct, the Pennine Way is joined for the next three miles, beginning by turning right along the short drive to Burnstones. *The fine three-storeyed house at the heart of this cluster was at one time the Burnstones Inn, evidenced by an old tablet on the porch wall referring to a former host Nichlos Moor.* Remain on the track turning right alongside the house to ascend steeply right, passing through a gate. Leveling out to pass through a gate onto the lower flanks of Glendue Fell, the track soon turns to climb away. *It is a modern bulldozed track onto the moors, built to allow shooting parties easier access to the grouse butts.* Ignore the track and go straight ahead, keeping just above the level wall on your right. At this stage largely pathless, head on past the hollow of an old quarry and rise slightly above the wall, avoiding some moist moments and picking up a slightly better path (the Maiden Way) running to a stile/gate in a wall ahead.

If you're wondering where the Pennine Way actually is, then voting with feet has seen it transfer unofficially onto the South Tyne Trail, below you! Decidedly older than the Pennine Way is the Roman road known as the Maiden Way, which linked forts at Kirkby Thore in the Eden Valley and Carvoran near Greenhead, in the shadow of Hadrian's Wall. You may have become aware of it on the approach to the last stile, and its course is now followed, by and large, for almost three miles. Head away, joining a track winding up from the barn below. Follow this briefly left until it turns to climb away, then again keep straight on, now on a better grassy track to a stile in the fence ahead. Advance to the next stile from where you are re-united with the wall. This leads a vastly improved path along the reedy yet largely dry edge of the common, a fine stride that gradually descends towards the valley of Glen Due.

Ahead is the last quarter of the walk, rising by a wall across the edge of heathery Hartleyburn Common. Still on the course of the Roman way, the path angles gently away from the wall again to reach a stile in a fence overlooking Glen Due. The path slants left down to the valley floor, to find a little footbridge a few yards upstream. Cross and consider a short break in this pleasing setting, less than half a mile upstream of your outward route over the Glendue Viaduct. From the stile in front rise right with the fence overlooking the road bridge. A wall quickly takes over, and above this short pull onto the edge of Hartleyburn Common, you are suddenly directed over a stile to trace the grassier environs east of the wall. Though harshly robbed of the heather moor, this proves a fine way as the thin path ascends into increasingly rougher surrounds of Lambley Common. This way, incidentally, remains your route all the way to the A689 just above Lambley, a dead-straight line shared with the Roman road to your left. Several stiles interrupt proceedings, but otherwise little description is needed.

On gaining the highest point at around 960ft/293m the wall is replaced by a fence: take care not to drop into a bog from the stile in your cross-fence. After a less than endearing hundred yards things rapidly improve again, and a long, gradual descent ensues. *Views by this stage stretch far and wide, out of the confines of the South Tyne valley to the ridge of Hadrian's Wall, and the dark, all-embracing forests beyond. In late summer all this is flavoured by the scent and colour of the adjacent heather. Lambley comes into view down to the right, and the river leads the eye downstream to locate isolated Featherstone Castle in its parkland setting.* With the road at Shanters Houses just ahead, the PW finally takes its leave by crossing the fence at a stile. Bid farewell and continue straight down a forming track to a gate onto the A689.

Cross with care to Shanters Houses. Down the road opposite, turn immediately along the end of the short row, along a garden side and on to a stile into a field. Head directly away to a stile in the fence ahead. *Down to the left are the remains of Lambley Colliery, while directly ahead is the church.* A thin path runs across an unkempt pasture to a kissing-gate in a wall, leading to a final field. *The embankment of the old mineral line is very distinct down to the left.*

Through a gate at the end use an underpass beneath the side road, which was only constructed in the 1970s to improve access to the isolated Coanwood area. At the other side an enclosed track runs on into Lambley, beneath the church. As it forks in front of a house, take the path bearing right to emerge onto the road in the tiny village centre. Turn right to finish, rising past the phone box and pleasantly appointed church (St Mary & St Patrick, 1885) to the main road.

Burnstones from the old viaduct

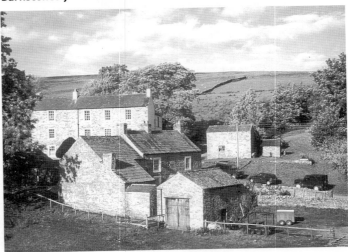

LAMBLEY VIADUCT

START *Coanwood*   *Grid ref.* **NY 679595**

DISTANCE 5¹4 miles (8¹2km)

ORDNANCE SURVEY MAPS
1:50,000
*Landranger 86 - Haltwhistle & Brampton **or***
Landranger 87 - Hexham & Haltwhistle
1:25,000
Explorer OL43 - Hadrian's Wall

ACCESS Start from Coanwood car park on the South Tyne Trail, just west of the village. Signed on roadsigns as 'Lambley Viaduct - South Tyne Trail'. Coanwood is served by bus from Haltwhistle.

> *A richly varied walk on both banks of the South Tyne, with an old rail track and fine woodland overshadowed by a crossing of the awesome old viaduct high above the river*

Begin by crossing the road and head off southwards along the South Tyne Trail, a super walk on the preserved course of the old railway through charming wooded surrounds. *The South Tyne Trail was created to provide a public walkway along the trackbed of the old Haltwhistle to Alston branch railway, a hugely successful enterprise which gives more than a dozen miles of level walking through superb, otherwise largely hidden scenery. The trail's final section to Alston is shared with the narrow-gauge railway which operates there - see WALK 8.* Passing an old house at the site of Coanwood Station, continue on past a couple of enviably sited houses enjoying big views over to the right. Very quickly and quite unexpectedly you arrive, already, at the walk's major highlight, Lambley Viaduct.

Cross slowly to savour this spectacular setting. *The viaduct was opened in 1852, providing the final link in the Newcastle & Carlisle Railway Company's branch line, which left the main line at Haltwhistle. Built of locally quarried stone it soars more than a hundred feet above the South Tyne, comprising nine main arches and seven smaller spans. The line's principal purpose in this sparsely populated area was to transport lead, coal and quarried limestone. Its value in serving small communities affected by snowblocked winter roads helped it survive as part of the national network until 1976, but the opening of the Lambley-Coanwood link road was the final nail in the coffin. Deterioration of the viaduct rapidly set in, and the sterling work of the North Pennines Heritage Trust was instrumental in its restoration some twenty years later. Today we are able to safely savour this remarkable situation and marvel at the engineering of this major landmark of the North Pennines. For a note on Lambley itself, see WALK 10.*

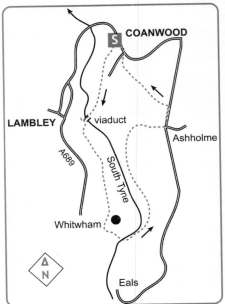

The far end greets you with an unexpected impasse, as the way is barred by private grounds. Instead, the path is sent down iron steps on the right to a path junction in the woods. Take that doubling back right, down again and passing under a side arch of the viaduct. By the lowest point you are almost at river level. The path however immediately turns to re-ascend, climbing wooden steps to run beneath Lambley's old station house, now restored as a private dwelling.

Running beneath the old buildings the line is rejoined, now shared by the driveway. *At this point look back to enjoy a fine prospect of the viaduct.* Advance on to a junction with an access road alongside a cottage. Cross straight over to a gate to resume along the old line, now a more user-friendly track. *This provides a splendid stride with fine views over the valley - keep an eye out for some interesting lineside carvings.*

After crossing the drive to Whitwham Farm, below, the track approaches Glendue Wood. Leave before this however, after a gate at an information panel, by taking steps dropping left to a stile off the embankment. A super little path descends colourful terrain alongside the Glendue Burn, crossing it lower down by a wooden footbridge and into an inviting clearing. Just a few steps further left is a sudden arrival at the River South Tyne. *This is found in a superbly characterful setting of rock, heather and scrub, very much a place to linger.*

Cross the footbridge over the river to join a track. Turn left on this, downstream to emerge via a stile into a field. Continue along this charming riverbank meadow to approach its terminus at the wooded bank ahead. *With a craggy wall just downstream, this is another grand spot before leaving the river.* To continue, cross a footbridge on the right into Towsbank Wood. A thin path slants left up the bank before levelling out to run a super course through trees high above the river. Rising a little more it merges with another path just short of a stile at a sidestream crossing. Continuing, now with the temporary company of a wall, the path soon finds itself at the top of the wood. Now with pastures above, it continues a level course along the wood top for a considerable time.

A dark hundred or so paces of a canopy of conifers signals the end as a forest track rises from the left, and there is no obvious continuation of the path. Take a gate on the right to finally leave the trees, and a super green track ascends a reedy pasture towards some farm buildings at the top. Ignore a ladder-stile on the left partway up, and remain on this same track after a ladder-stile into a second pasture. *You can now take in a sweeping panorama back to the viaduct and extensive surroundings.* At the very top corner is a gate/stile by the farm buildings at Ashholme. Joining a farm road, go a few paces left to meet a through road, and keep left along it.

Ashholme's nice little stone terrace once featured a pub, while unchanged ahead from the walk's high point at around 900ft/274m is an extensive panorama leading the eye to Hadrian's Wall country, while Cold Fell, the Pennines' northernmost 2000-footer, rises to the west. The road is soon left where footpaths depart to both sides. From a gate on the left head directly away to a brow, and as the wall on the right curves away, bear gently right to meet the fence ahead. Now turn right to descend a dry, reedy pasture alongside the fence, on a fine green way with good views ahead. When the fence turns off, continue down between two stands of trees, with Coanwood just ahead.

Maintain this slant to drop to a gate in a fence ahead, side-stepping a reedy corner just before it. Continue down to a wooden farm bridge and advance to the buildings ahead, the former village Post office. Turn left on the access track past the main barn to a gate to its left, then follow the enclosed driveway away to emerge onto a side road (the old station road) in Coanwood. *This small, scattered community retains its school which absorbs young pupils from an extensive rural area.* Turn right the short way to the through road, then go left down it for a couple of minutes back to the car park.

Lambley Viaduct

FEATHERSTONE PARK

START *Featherstone* Grid ref. *NY 681607*

DISTANCE *5 miles (8km)*

ORDNANCE SURVEY MAPS
1:50,000
Landranger 86 - Haltwhistle & Brampton or
Landranger 87 - Hexham & Haltwhistle
1:25,000
Explorer OL43 - Hadrian's Wall

ACCESS *Start from Featherstone Park Station car park on the South Tyne Trail, by the hamlet of Featherstone Rowfoot some three miles south-west of Haltwhistle. Buses from Haltwhistle.*

> *Idyllic parkland and an old railway are augmented by lovely riverbank, grandiose castle and prison camp*

Featherstone Rowfoot, to use its full name, is a tiny settlement historically linked to Featherstone Castle which sits on riverside meadows in the valley below. It lost its station as recently as 1976 when the Alston branch line closed, but currently it retains the lifeline of a pub, the white-walled Wallace Arms. Its name recalls a family that occupied the castle in Victorian times.

From the car park gain the line, but immediately abandon the railway and cross the road at the former level crossing, passing the station house on your right. Almost at once a path turns off through a stile on the right into woodland. It runs outside the garden to reach a stile at the end. Turn sharp left outside the wood and up the fenceside to a stile into a vast open sheep pasture, a very pleasant part of the Featherstone Castle parkland. Head away, bearing slightly right to a fence-stile and on again to a stile ahead.

Now cross a similar pasture to another stile, then bear left to a stile into the extensive wood ahead. A good path runs to a small clearing beneath a distinctive large beech tree, and with a steep bank on the left, it descends wooden steps to emerge at a stile at the bottom. A fine prospect ahead features Featherstone Bridge. Head directly away to an intervening stile, and straight on to a stile onto the road at Bridge End. *This is a superb setting, with the old bridge climbing steeply to the South Tyne's wooded bank. It dates from 1778, its predecessor having been consumed by flood.*

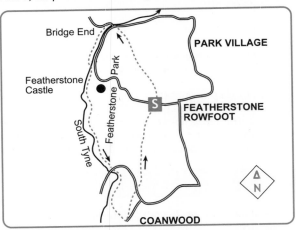

Cross the bridge and rise away, but quickly leave by a path into trees on the left. This runs well above the river before gradually dropping to join it. The path continues at this lower level to a footbridge on inflowing Glencune Burn. Continuing, the path suddenly arrives at a footbridge on the river, which is crossed. *While upon it you can still espy Featherstone Bridge downstream, while beneath your feet, great slabs of rock make a very firm riverbed.*

Across, turn immediately upstream: there is little point in taking the stile onto the back road. Here begins an idyllic section, though first you will wish to pause to appraise Featherstone Castle impressively planted in the centre of its pastoral parkland. *Though largely rebuilt in the early 1800s by the Wallace family, this grand* house incorporates the remains of a 14th century tower surviving through many centuries of use by the Featherstonehaugh family. After a couple of mid-20th century decades as a school, it is again a private residence. Annual ghostly sightings supposedly recall the legend of the Bride of Featherstonehaugh. The maiden in question was due to fulfil her father's wish to marry, but while the wedding party was undertaking a ritual riding of the bounds, they were ambushed by her desperate lover: things went awry when she was accidentally killed, causing the young man to take his own life: ultimately there were no survivors, as her father discovered when the group finally returned to the house, but in spirit only!

Head along the grassy bank, past fine beeches scattered around this archetypal parkland. After passing a weir, you soon merge into an old track which remains underfoot all the way along this splendid bank of the wide-flowing South Tyne. The site of former sewage works is passed to arrive at the more intriguing site of a Second World War prison camp. *Alongside extensive foundations stand largely intact red-brick huts. Close by is a watchtower. Note with some caution, hereabouts, the dramatic effects of erosion of the bank where the old tarmac track has collapsed into the river.*

Resume upstream, still on a track which runs on through a gate and on to approach the charmless concrete of Coanwood Bridge, swinging left to rise to a gate onto the road just before it. *The bridge was built in the 1970s to facilitate a new road link from Coanwood out to the A689 at Lambley. Whilst opening new access from remote communities to the outside world, it also effectively ended the area's reliance on the railway.* Cross the road but not the bridge, and just a few steps to the right another track heads off from a gate. This drops back to regain the riverbank in a lovely corner, then fades as you resume upstream into open surrounds. A tiny trickling stream deflects steps away from the river, to a bridge of sorts alongside clumps of scrub. Across, a thin path bears left, rising to a restored house just ahead. Its drive then leads steeply up the bank to the old railway at the site of Coanwood station.

Turn left on the line leading unfailingly back to Featherstone Park Station. The first section is through woodland that suddenly reveals a fine view over the valley. Further, the 'new' Coanwood road is crossed to Coanwood car park. Resume along the line to enjoy a glorious finale on a largely delectably greensward.

BROOMHOUSE COMMON

START *Featherstone*   *Grid ref.* **NY 681607**

DISTANCE *5³4 miles (9km)*

ORDNANCE SURVEY MAPS
1:50,000
Landranger 86 - Haltwhistle & Brampton **or**
Landranger 87 - Hexham & Haltwhistle
1:25,000
Explorer OL43 - Hadrian's Wall

ACCESS *Start from Featherstone Park Station car park on the South Tyne Trail, by the hamlet of Featherstone Rowfoot some three miles south-west of Haltwhistle. Served by bus from Haltwhistle.*

> *A remarkable catalogue of features are sprinkled along this ramble, including riverbank, old railway, woodland, waterfalls, and best of all the open spaces of Broomhouse Common*

Featherstone Rowfoot, to use its full name, is a tiny settlement historically linked to Featherstone Castle which sits on riverside meadows in the valley below. It lost its station as recently as 1976 when the Alston branch line closed, but currently it retains the lifeline of a pub, the white-walled Wallace Arms. Its name recalls a family that occupied the castle in Victorian times.

From the car park join the line, cross the road and head north past the old station house and platform. *The Trail was created to provide a public walkway along the trackbed of the old Haltwhistle to Alston branch railway, which gives more than a dozen miles of level walking through superb, otherwise hidden scenery.* Emerging from a cutting the track runs into trees, and onto a high embankment over the beautiful wooded environs of Park Burn, of which more later. Across, the wooded gill remains on the left and the track runs on to approach Park Village. Turn left up a broad path before the bridge to rise to a gate onto the road at the top end of the village. Turn left down the winding street. *Park Village is little more than a hamlet, consisting of a few cottages and a former Wesleyan chapel and schoolroom of 1850. Happily it has long been by-passed by the through road.* At the bottom of the street the roads merge. Continue a little further and then locate a stile set back on the right. In the field go left to a ladder-stile, then rise diagonally across a large field to a gate at the far corner.

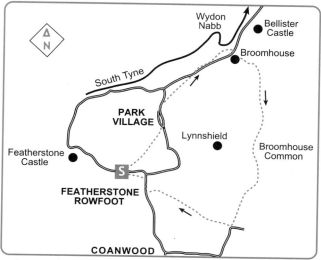

Go very briefly right along the road, above a colourful slope dropping to the presently unseen South Tyne. Ahead is Haltwhistle. As the bank ends take a stile on the left and resume on the other side of the wall. As the road turns away, drop left with the embanked field boundary, with the river rushing below Wydon Nabb ahead. The fence slants down to the tapering corner where a stile admits into the woods high above the river. Turn right on a good path, springtime bluebells adding to a splendid short interlude high above a steep wooded bank, caution! *Gaps in the trees permit super views over the South Tyne's wide, stony course. This sharp bend is backed by the crumbly scar of Wydon Nabb.* Just beyond a viewpoint seat the path swings down to the left, but instead use a short path to the right to meet the road climbing Bellister Bank.

Turn uphill for a couple of minutes to the bend at Broomhouse, and go left along the enclosed driveway keeping left of the farm buildings. *These form a most impressive arrangement, with a fine circular addition to the rear of an immense old barn.* The track passes through a gate on the left and heads away between walls to a bridge over the old railway, and thus the South Tyne Trail, again. The now grassy track heads away to a gate onto a corner of Broomhouse Common. The track rises to a wall corner. Remain on this old way as it turns right then sharply left uphill again just yards further, ignoring a lesser branch right. This now makes a splendid short ascent to the brow above, a comfortable greensward amid the tussocks. *On the brow, grassy banks just to the right identify the site of an Iron Age settlement. One can discern its outer walls - with some stone evident - while inside are circular enclosures, with a particularly prominent one of some 30ft diameter.*

The path runs clearly on, dropping to cross a small side stream and rising to a fork just up the other side. From this point on you may encounter a potentially confusing array of branch paths and some waymarks: it's not really that complicated, you're basically heading south above a small side valley to your left. Keep left above the minor stream, and remain on this way as another fork goes right. The way fades at a brow as you look down on the head of this side valley, with a small rocky area below and a better one further ahead (neither of which you visit, however!). Here a clear path swings right, slanting down to a junction where keep straight on, curving round to cross another tiny sidestream and onto a brow, where the thin but clear way forks above a deep hollow. While the left one drops into the hollow near a solitary boulder, opt to keep right on the level path running towards the broad gap at its head.

Although the path fades, simply head on through the gap, and with a new view opening ahead, forge straight on to drop gently to a sudden arrival above a sweeping bend of the Park Burn. This proves a dramatic spot as the moor falls away to a colourful riot at your feet. This is but the first half of the drama: turn left on the thin path above the rim of this steep bank, a delectable, all-too-brief stroll to an equally stunning moment. Looking down from this heathery knoll the perfect scene now features a cascading waterfall; all in all a combination of rock, bracken, heather, gorse and water fusing into one little piece of heaven. *Caution - if venturing down to the bank, there's a small crag below you at this point.*

Resuming, the little path runs to a stile/gate in the wall just ahead, from where a good path heads off through heather. Keeping to the now tamer bank above the burn, it steers a fairly clear course: towards the end the heather fades, simply remain on the track which runs to a waiting footbridge. Its length certainly caters for the occasions when the Park Burn might be in spate. Across, a track rises from the adjacent ford to a gate off the common. A good track heads away between trees, a dead straight course to reach a bend on a back road. Don't join it but take a stile on the right, and head away over pathless rough pasture. This is the first of several, some being a little moist and with fences that never found their way onto the map. Merge with the fence to the right to cross it by a stile part way on, then bear gently away from it.

Your objective is the right-hand side of the skyline clump of trees, and the invisible path strikes a direct course through an old wall to a fence-stile, and on again to one at an old wall corner before a change of terrain as you ascend the dry grassy slope to the brow. *At around 725ft/221m this is the walk's modest high point: it offers a view north to the Whin Sill ridge supporting Hadrian's Wall; north-west to the vast forests beyond, and west (straight ahead) to the unkempt commons across the South Tyne.* Keep on past the trees and down to the very far corner, where a stile is defended by a moist area featuring a reedy pool.

Head diagonally away over a rough but dry hummocky pasture, through tracts of gorse and past another pool to drop to another corner stile. Across, go left along the wallside down to a stile onto a road alongside a lone house. Turn right for Featherstone Rowfoot, just two minutes away. The nicest finish escapes the road, and just short of the junction take a driveway down to the left, ending at an attractive cluster of cottages. Keep left of all buildings on a grassy way to a gate, and descend the fieldside. Partway, a convenient stile gives access to the pub, otherwise continue further down as far as a kissing-gate onto the road just above the car park.

14

STAWARD PEEL

START *Allen Banks*   Grid ref. *NY 798640*

DISTANCE *6¼ miles (10km)*

ORDNANCE SURVEY MAPS
1:50,000
Landranger 86 - Haltwhistle & Brampton or
Landranger 87 - Hexham & Haltwhistle
1:25,000
Explorer OL43 - Hadrian's Wall

ACCESS *Start from the National Trust's Allen Banks car park signed off the A69 a mile east of Bardon Mill, adjacent to Ridley Hall. Newcastle-Carlisle buses serve the main road.*

> *A splendid ramble through a wooded gorge, with the fascinating objective of an ancient hilltop tower. Some sections are on National Trust permissive paths*

The woodland and gorges of Allen Banks were part of the estate of adjacent Ridley Hall, and were transformed into a more formal 'wilderness walking' area by the then occupants during the mid 19th century. The area was handed to the National Trust in 1942, and they produce an informative leaflet which is available locally, usually on site.

From the end of the car park a broad path heads into the trees, immediately joining forces with the River Allen to head upstream. This is a superb, level walk through delightful scenery, the river lively and the woodland varied. Don't expect to be alone though, for it is rightly popular. Ignore any branches turning off, and remain on the bank to arrive at a dramatically suspended foot-bridge. The walk shall return to this point by crossing that bridge!

For now continue upstream, soon reaching a shapely bend overlooked by fine rock walls on the opposite bank. River and path swing right here, passing beneath the weirdly naturally sculpted rock walls of Raven Crag. The path then climbs and undulates through the wooded slopes before dropping back towards the bank. At a ruin, National Trust land is traded for Briarwood Banks. *This is a nature reserve of the Northumberland Wildlife Trust, an ancient woodland comprising oak, ash and hazel coppice.* Continue a little further over a footbridge on a sidestream: up the other side the main path forks right to suddenly reach another suspension bridge on the Allen. This time cross, to reach the farm at Plankey Mill on the other bank.

The walk returns to this point, giving the immediate option of joining it now for a short return. First, however, is the spectacular loop to visit Staward Peel. Turn upstream through a stile to enjoy a stroll through a lovely riverside pasture, and just short of the end bear left to a stile into woodland. Here a broad track runs upstream into the deeply wooded Staward Gorge. Note the impressive river-level crags. The main path leaves the river, rises away a little, then drops back down and over a footbridge on a sidestream to a fork. Branch left, very quickly forking again. Take the path to the left, which commences a very steep but profitable climb, to suddenly find itself at the surviving walls of Staward Peel.

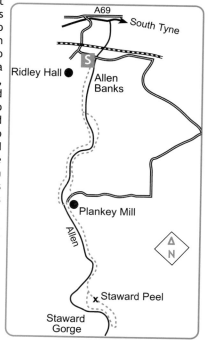

In this impressive setting are the remains of one of countless fortified houses built in the Border counties to deter unwelcome visitors from the north. Dating from the late 13th century it became an idyllic retreat for monks from a Hexham priory until the Dissolution in the 1530s. A good path continues away, passing the small free-standing remnant of a gatehouse. From nowhere a ridge takes shape, quickly emerging into a quite dramatic situation as the narrowest point of this slender tongue is reached at some rocky outcrops. *This is a superb moment, a place to sit awhile and look over the deep woodland of the Staward Gorge winding far below.*

Advancing just a little further, and with a gate out of the woods visible ahead, instead bear right on a thinner path. This runs pleasantly along the wood top for a few minutes, to reach a gate/stile in the wall on the left. Here turn right on a broad path slanting down into the woods. It doubles back right and drops pleasantly down to a junction, still high above the river. Here keep right, continuing the straight, steady descent towards the valley floor. Approaching an old gateway, don't pass through but turn right with the wall and then remain with it, sharp left and along to rejoin the outward path at the foot of the steep pull to the peel. Now advance straight on to retrace steps to the farm at Plankey Mill.

Back at Plankey Mill turn right on the access road climbing away. After a steep pull escape left on a permissive path along a cart track. This runs on high above the river, but quickly take a stile on the left. A path heads away directly above the river, and soon ends with a stile over a wall into an open pasture. Continue with a fence, dropping down at the end to a stile where a wall takes over to rejoin the riverbank proper. The path now provides a splendid ramble along the bank enclosed by a wall. Ending at a wooded bank, a stile and bridge lead back into trees. The path rises left beneath crags to give a choice of ways back to the suspension bridge passed early in the walk. *Easiest option remains on the lower path.*

At an early fork, the right-hand path doubles back up a stone stairway to the right to plot a splendid course beneath rocky cliffs. At a fork turn down to the left, onto a lower path still well above the river. Go right, rising a little beneath an impressive crag, then at the next fork go left again, now dropping to the riverbank by the bridge. An exhilarating crossing leads back to the outward path, which you can again enjoy as it leads back to the start.

15

MO HOPE VALLEY

START *Ninebanks*   *Grid ref.* NY 782524

DISTANCE *4³4 miles (7¹2km)*

ORDNANCE SURVEY MAPS
1:50,000
Landranger 86 - Haltwhistle & Brampton *or*
Landranger 87 - Hexham & Haltwhistle
1:25,000
Explorer OL43 - Hadrian's Wall

ACCESS *Start from the Carrshield road by the church. Limited parking. An on-route alternative start is a small parking area across Blackpool Bridge, down a side road (signed Alston/Mohope) from the junction north of the church. The start is best reached by turning off the A686 1¹2 miles south of Whitfield. Served by occasional Alston/Nenthead-Allendale/Hexham bus, also Hexham-Alston bus service one mile away on the A686.*

An undemanding exploration of the little known valley of Mo Hope as it merges into similarly unfrequented West Allen Dale

Ninebanks is a scattered settlement in the valley of the West Allen. St Mark's church was rebuilt in 1871 and has a spire on a small turret. A good half-mile north is Ninebanks' modest hub, with a fine four-storey, 16th century Tower facing a tiny green. The remote youth hostel is a mile south-west at Keirsleywell Row. Based in an old miner's cottage, it is one of the country's oldest surviving hostels, having welcomed travellers since 1948.

Start by heading north down the road, very quickly doubling back left on a path down the small wooded bank to the lower road. Go left to cross Blackpool Bridge on the River West Allen. Turn left past the alternative parking area on the cul-de-sac road running south, signed to Farney Shield. This runs a pleasant level course, largely in company with the West Allen. Partway on is the notable confluence with the Mohope Burn, of which more very shortly. Just a little further is Malakoff Bridge on the river. Don't cross it, but take a gate on the right and head upstream by the Mohope Burn. *In this region a 'hope' is a valley - pronounced 'up'.* This offers a nice stroll along the grassy bank, through a gate in a wall then on to a wooded bank on a possibly dry bend of the stream.

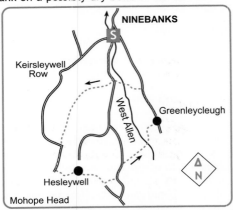

Here the Mohope Burn is abandoned. A path runs through the few trees, but then cross a tiny sidestream and ascend the grassy bank ahead, with the stream down to your right. A faint path might be traced along the crest, with a wooded bank dropping to the right. Maintain this line through a ladder-stile, and on a further field bearing slightly right: towards the end you have a wooded bank on both sides. Pass through a gate and forge on along the abating ridge, bound for a house ahead. Advance through a gateway in a wall and on to the house. From a stile in front, pass along the house front and out to a gate onto a narrow back road. Go left, past one house and along to the isolated phone box at Nether House.

As the road bends away after the buildings, pass through a gateway on the left and descend to a footbridge on the Mohope Burn. Furtively hidden in this charming corner is the ruin of

The old chapel, Appletree Shield

Appletree Shield's early 19th century Primitive Methodist chapel. *This religion thrived in lead mining areas, and this was the first purpose built chapel in the area in 1820, rebuilt and then closed in 1870s after a miners' exodus. Though seemingly tucked away, it was centrally sited for the scattered Mohope inhabitants.* Round the back is a bigger footbridge on the Wellhope Burn, flowing through an impressively rocky gorge. Across, a path bears left, quickly scaling a wooded bank to a bridle-gate at the top. Bear left up the field to ascend to the farm at Hesleywell above. Take the gate between two large barns into the yard, and straight up to the road end just above. Go right a few yards and take a wall-stile just above to climb the steep field. At the top is a wall-stile well to the right of a ruined farmhouse. This admits onto an access track.

Bear left through a gate to an open area. This stands on the crest of the declining ridge dividing the last mile of the Mohope Burn from its confluence with the West Allen. Now slant left down through a gateway to a house. Pass to its right and bear right to a stile out of the garden, continuing with the hedge on the right down through further stiles to emerge into an open field with the house at Broadlee just below. Maintain the slant down by a tiny stream, crossing it to a gate in the wall at the bottom onto a back road. Go left past the house, and just beyond a bend take a stile on the right. Head along the fieldside by a belt of trees, and from a stile at the end a grassy track drops down a reedy pasture to a stile/gate at the bottom. A rutted track descends the bank to the riverside pasture, bear left to a footbridge on the West Allen.

Across, go left along the base of the wooded bank to a tiny footbridge, then ascend a steep path through trees. At the top climb a steep field to a stile, then up one final one to the farm of Greenley Cleugh, with a wooded clough on your right. Pass right of the buildings to a stile onto a road. The farmhouse bears a 1689 datestone. Go left for a nice stroll with good views of the route thus far. Past the house at Farneyside and then some cottages, take a stile on the left to descend a field alongside a tree-lined stream. Levelling out at the bottom, bear right to a footbridge re-crossing the West Allen. At the other side, the path runs to a stile then rise up the fieldside, but before the brow bear right to a stile onto a back road. Drop right to emerge back at Malakoff Bridge, crossing it to retrace opening steps back along the road to the start.

Whiteley Shield, Carrshield, West Allen Dale

16

WEST ALLEN DALE

START *Carrshield*   *Grid ref.* **NY 803475**

DISTANCE *4³⁄4 miles (7¹⁄2km)*

ORDNANCE SURVEY MAPS
1:50,000
Landranger 86 - Haltwhistle & Brampton **or**
Landranger 87 - Hexham & Haltwhistle
1:25,000
Explorer OL31 - North Pennines (Teesdale/Weardale)

ACCESS *Start from the hamlet on the Nenthead-Allendale Town road. Roadside parking. Served by occasional Alston-Hexham bus.*

> *A quiet corner of West Allen Dale is the scene for this varied walk on riverbank, rough pasture and with its share of history*

Carrshield is a small community, little more than a hamlet off the beaten track in secluded West Allen Dale. From the small open area just south of the phone box, turn down a few steps and down a lawn amid haphazardly arranged cottages. At the bottom a path slants left down to a gate in front of a footbridge on the West Allen. Without crossing the bridge take a stile on the right, and along to another stile just beyond. A tight little way runs on to escape into a field, to head downstream with the youthful river in more comfortable surroundings. Map and path are not in complete accord here, so stay near the river to pass through a gate beneath the start of a wooded bank. Simply remain on the bank to reach a gateway in an old wall, with a footbridge waiting just ahead.

Cross the river and an old stone stairway ascends the steep grassy bank, then advance to the fence corner just ahead. Go right with the fence as far as a stile in it, then cross the meadow behind towards the buildings of Black Cleugh Farm. *From here you can enjoy some splendid views down the dale.* A gate in front of the buildings gives access, passing straight through and out of a gate at the other end, on the access road. Leave this almost at once (after passing a small fenced enclosure) by a gate on the left. From here an inviting grassy way slants up the meadow towards a barn, Blackcleugh, at the top corner. Take a gate in front of the barn and pass round the back, where further gates give access to the rough moorland of Bottoms.

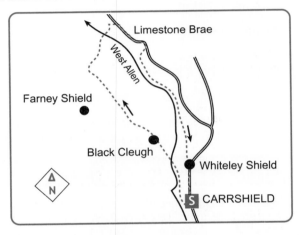

Turn right along the wallside, the first few minutes being exceptionally reedy but not particularly damp. The going soon improves as you trace the moor edge along, crossing deep-cut Pattison's Sike and on to encounter a much deeper crossing, with caution as a steep shaley bank guards it. Slant down around it and resume towards a barn at the end. Up above is the farm at Farney Shield. Leave before the barn, however, by a gate in the adjacent wall with a sheep pen just over it.

A grassy track drops down the wallside of this reedy pasture. *Again there are good views down the valley to a moorland skyline.* Part way down, a farm track takes over to lead down to a foot-bridge and ford on the West Allen. Cross to the gate behind and ascend the steeply winding track. Passing through a gate level with a house, don't advance onto its drive but take a stile on the right, and ascend a steep field to a top corner stile onto a road alongside a cemetery.

Turn right on here, a nice stroll with grand views over most of the route backed by the high moorland of The Dodd (see WALK 17). Just ahead, at Limestone Brae, you pass an old Methodist Chapel of 1825, with a Sunday School attached fifty years later. *A more modern (for England!) religious scene is presented by the adjacent Throssel Hole Buddhist Abbey, which displays its opening times on the information board.* Continue on into the deep wooded gill of Wolf Cleugh. Coming out the other side, take a stile on the right and descend the fieldside outside the trees to rejoin the river. In front are a footbridge and the ruin of an old mill.

Ignore the footbridge and turn upstream for a delightful ramble, traces of a grassy mill-race leading a hundred yards to a delectable corner where the youthful river tumbles over rocky shelves of angular blocks. Resuming, remain by the river all the way to a farm bridge on it, which is not crossed. Instead, forsake the West Allen and ascend a few yards up the farm track to the left, but quickly rise right above a wooded side gill. Part way up, a little path slants into the few trees to find a footbridge on the tiny stream. Across, another set of old stone steps ascend a grassy bank, from where rise pathless to the wall above. Take a bridle-gate in it and resume alongside the wall to the right, leading through three pastures to approach the farm at Whiteley Shield.

Enter at a gate in front of the first barn, and follow the track out past various barns. *In the first group of buildings a gable end wall on the right displays a former arched doorway: this is the remains of a bastle, a fortified farmhouse of the 16th century.* Past the attractive farm cottage the road is rejoined. Continue along this to finish. *En route you pass Whiteley Shield Primitive Methodist Chapel of 1857, before the luxury of a pavement into the hamlet. On the left is the former school, a tablet proclaiming 'Car Shield school built by and on land belonging to W B Beaumont Esq for the education of children of all religious denominations 1851'. The benefactor's name is significant in that the influential Blackett-Beaumont family ran most of the lead mining operations in the Allendale area.*

17

THE DODD

START *Carrshield*   *Grid ref.* NY 803475

DISTANCE 5$\frac{1}{2}$ miles (9km)

ORDNANCE SURVEY MAPS
1:50,000
Landranger 86 - Haltwhistle & Brampton **or**
Landranger 87 - Hexham & Haltwhistle
1:25,000
Explorer OL31 - North Pennines (Teesdale/Weardale)

ACCESS Start from the hamlet on the Nenthead-Allendale Town road. Roadside parking. Served by occasional Alston/Nenthead-Allendale/Hexham buses.

A circuit of Smallburns Moor giving a rare easy opportunity to visit a 2000ft summit. Although never that remote or wild, and with good terrain underfoot, it nevertheless needs a clear day

Carrshield is a small community, little more than a hamlet off the beaten track in secluded West Allen Dale. From the small open area just south of the phone box, turn down a few steps and down a lawn amid haphazardly arranged cottages. At the bottom a path slants left down to a gate in front of a footbridge on the West Allen. Across, ascend the steep little bank, then continue up the reedy pasture on a decent track. From a gate in the top fence rise a few yards further to meet the access road to Smallburns. *Just to the right stands a well-preserved limekiln.*

Cross straight over and up an inviting grassy track onto Smallburns Moor. This rises splendidly alongside a wall, with a tree-shrouded stream just over it. Higher, pass a sheep-pen and continue up until the wall parts company. Here the path largely gives up the ghost too. The route is waymarked by the occasional post as it slants up to the right. A faint trod may be found but it remains reasonable going, soon easing out to reach a bridleway crossroads on the broad moorland ridge. This otherwise grand spot is marred by the presence of a tall wooden guidepost. *Excellent all-round views include a big skyline west to the high Pennine watershed, and north down the valley towards Hadrian's Wall country.*

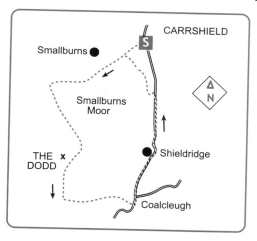

Turn left on a clear grassy track, ascending very gently and savouring every invigorating step. Two similar tracks are absorbed, one from the left then one from the right. The grassy way runs southwards to skirt the summit plateau of The Dodd. At this altitude and proximity this is a rare opportunity to claim a 2000ft mountain summit. Don't jump the gun, however, but remain on the bridleway as it contours round the flank. After passing a string of modern grouse butts down to the left, consider the detour up the faintly heathery bank on your right, almost at once revealing the summit cairn a short distance away. It sits rather forlornly amid modest peat groughs and cotton grass, but given that someone at some point made the effort to cart the stones here, it seems only right to visit the place.

At 2014ft/614m The Dodd is an innocuous swell of moorland rising between the upper waters of the Rivers Nent and West Allen. While it sends rolling moors stretching north between the two valleys, it is swiftly cut off to the south by slopes rising to the watershed with the Wear. Probably of most interest in the view is the prospect of neighbouring Killhope Law's dome to the south-east across the West Allen's headwaters, while more distantly Cross Fell and its acolytes form a lofty skyline to the south-west.

Back on the bridleway resume as before, the route only fading at Dodd's End as it approaches a wall. Bear right toward the wall and then left on a good grassy way running just downhill alongside it. At a bridle-gate in the wall, just before a fence takes over, is another junction. Ignore the gate and go directly left away from it, a path rapidly transforming into a splendid route as it drops gently down alongside a stream. Towards the bottom the objective of Coalcleugh awaits. The path becomes a grassy old miners' track as it winds down to meet a firmer track amid mining remains. Turn right on this, over a modest ravine, through a gate and out past the newly renovated cottage at Sunnyside. Crossing a stream alongside a blocked mine level, the track slants up to the road at Coalcleugh.

From the mid 18th century Coalcleugh was a busy lead mining site with lead ore brought out of the Barney Craig Level by horse-drawn waggon on wooden rails. Primitive Methodists held services in the mineshop (where the men who lived some distance away lodged during their working week), very much preaching 'on-site'. The road is joined at a junction where the road from Nenthead forks for either Allenheads or Allendale Town.

Turn left down the quiet road with extensive views over West Allen Dale. *A lone house passed at Shieldridge has a datestone of 1826 and its own wind turbine. Further are two old quarry sites.* The road is vacated where a bridleway turns down by a fence on the left to join a hard drive. Double back on this over a cattle-grid and down to bridge the West Allen alongside an old mine building. *As the rough road doubles back out from the bridge note the dark adit, built to help drain water from the mines, still disgorging a fair supply.* The track runs above an extensive mining site and on past the isolated house of Barney Crag to meet the outward route in front of the gate by the limekiln. Turn right, down through the gate to return by way of the reedy pasture and footbridge.

18

ALLENDALE COMMON

START *Allenheads*   Grid ref. *NY 860453*

DISTANCE *6$\frac{1}{2}$ miles (10$\frac{1}{2}$km)*

ORDNANCE SURVEY MAPS
1:50,000
Landranger 87 - Hexham & Haltwhistle
1:25,000
Explorer OL31 - North Pennines (Teesdale / Weardale)

ACCESS *Start from the village centre. Several roadside parking areas off the road above, and the Heritage Centre has its own car park. Served by bus from Hexham via Allendale Town.*

Allendale Common is the name given to the massive sweeps of moorland on either side of the upper Allen valley. This walk also extends to both sides of the dale, combining outstanding moorland views with various lead mining interests and a delectable stroll along the infant River East Allen

Allenheads is an old lead mining community which lives up to its name, situated between 1350 and 1400 feet up at the very head of Allendale. While the Quaker-backed London Lead Company largely controlled mining in Alston Moor, the Allendale area was similarly run by the Blackett-Beaumont family. At its heart is a Heritage Centre featuring much of interest from lead mining days, and incorporates a Post office / shop and coffee shop. Alongside in the little square is the Armstrong engine house, displaying the massive hydraulic engine dating from 1846 that once supplied the village's electricity. Facing it is the Allenheads Inn, a splendidly characterful pub dating from 1770 which is virtually a museum in itself. The large building at the crossroads above the centre is the *former mine office: across from it is the deep circular Gin Hill shaft, which reached a depth of 240ft in order to access five separate horizontal levels. From this junction two roads climb out of the dalehead, one to Rookhope, the other to Cowshill in Weardale.*

Whilst the devastation of a century and a half of frenzied mining activity is evident all around the valley, perhaps harder to imagine is the impact on the population. The main collapse of the market came in the 1870s, due to a combination of cheap foreign imports, and the fact that much of the more accessible lead had already been taken out. Severe unemployment led to an exodus of thousands of dalesfolk, many to start new lives in America.

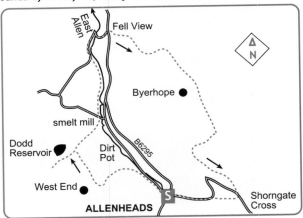

From the square outside the Heritage Centre, turn up a rough road at the top end of the pub. This rises to a sharp bend alongside cottages, where turn right along a driveway, rising slightly. Running on, when it starts to drop right towards a house, go straight on a path beneath trees. Merging into a forest track this runs on to quickly meet another driveway junction. Advance a few yards but don't go through the gate to the house beyond, instead turn up the near side of the fence on this path ascending the edge of a modest sidestream. A little higher, at the corner of the plantation, cross the stile and continue straight up, squeezed tightly by trees a very short way to reach a contouring path.

Turn right on this through the trees of School Plantation, now pleasantly non-claustrophobic, and soon reaching the edge. Over another stile the path runs freely on a fence-side outside the trees, with a wall below and grand views down Allendale. Keep on to the end, swinging left to a stile in the wall. Entering a field keep left: ahead is a moorland sweep of Allendale Common. Approaching a corner bear slightly right to a crumbling wall corner, and continue with the wall to a stile in the corner fence. Now turn left with the wall on a contouring path that soon merges into the driveway below. Continue along the farm drive as it curves in around the Westend Burn, but as it slants back out to a gate, leave it by keeping to the right side of the fence, resuming along the field top.

Pass by a small barn and down to a facing stile, then a thin trod maintains this course down the fieldsides, past the ruin of Viewly Hall. This is just one of numerous abandoned farms spread around. The final wallside runs down to a stile in the bottom corner accessing the open moor. Just to the right a grassy track drops down to cross tiny Blackcleugh Burn, then slants enjoyably back up the other side to join the firm track of the Carriers' Way. Although the route turns right, this old way is too good to short-change, so consider briefly extending the walk by turning left on it. This enjoys a near level stride across the moor. *The track can be seen climbing to the moortop, with the big cairn on Killhope Law prominent on the skyline further right. There are in fact two ways underfoot here, the old packhorse route paralleled by a flue rising from a smelt mill on the riverbank.*

On turning about, further variation can be added by rising for two minutes across the moor to the bank of the attractive Dodd Reservoir, which also served the lead mines. From its dam drop back to the Carriers' Way and continue downhill. Towards the bottom, as it swings left a nicer green track continues straight down, tracing the line of the flue to the forlorn remains of Allenheads Smelt Mill. *An important aspect of the lead mining process was the smelting of the lead, which involved heating the ore to produce a molten metal. The problem of the harmful fumes of the sulphur produced was resolved by the construction of substantial stone flues to carry the fumes safely away.* Just past it, a gate admits onto the road alongside the sturdy Old Smelt Mill Bridge of 1926. *Across it is the old main road that runs through Dirt Pot and back to Allenheads. For a swift return to Allenheads, cross the bridge and turn right along the road through Dirt Pot, passing some nice cottages, a Victorian postbox, a former Wesleyan Chapel of 1900, a redundant cast-iron pump and Allenheads Lodge, an outdoor centre.*

Don't cross the bridge, but go a few yards left up the road and then take a path signed off to the right. This runs faintly on the open common. Ignore a branch left to a driveway, and instead bear right on an improving path through heather on the crest of the modest bank well above the East Allen. Towards the end drop right to the bank of the river to avoid marshy ground, and the path squeezes between wall and river (the map suggests it runs through fields to the left). *Here begins a truly delightful section: gifted in season with flowery banks, the ambitiously titled river is just a tinkling stream.* A footbridge leads over inflowing Middlehope Burn alongside an old weir, and a little further ignore a footbridge on the river itself. This super walk leads on past the attractive grouping at Peasmeadows across the river, and at the end the path runs into trees to emerge onto a back road. Advance along this to reach a ford on the river at Huntwell. If the water level is forbidding then use the footbridge just ahead. Across, the road ascends steeply to meet the B6295 alongside a short row of cottages at Fell View.

Cross straight over to a gate and rise to a bridle-gate just above. You are now on the moorland flank of Allendale Common. A grassy track climbs away, its clear course zealously confirmed by waymarks as old quarry workings are passed. The delightful grassy path is a joy every step of the way as it offers an undemanding ascent of the similarly grassy moor, slanting to the right at times to break up the direct climb. *Pause to savour excellent views across the valley, with green pastures and scattered farms beneath the domed top of Killhope Law with its big summit cairn discernible: the old flue coming down to the smelt mill is clearly seen, while towards the top, the Dodd Reservoir also appears.* The path gains the level edge of Byerhope Bank to join a bulldozed shooters' track, a harsh eyesore after the lovely path you have just followed.

Turn right on this to disconcertingly start to descend. It's only brief, however, as you quickly reach a junction by a circular cairn. Bear left here, and all that remains is to keep to this track which can be seen far ahead. It meets the intake wall, running on above Byerhope Farm in its own little side valley which severs you from the main dale. Beyond a barn conversion the track climbs up and round to a 7ft tall currick that has long been prominent. *This imposing cairn stands on a heathery mound and is the perfect Allenheads viewpoint, giving a surprise view of the village almost at your feet. Perhaps most remarkable is the almost suffocating surround of plantations. Note also the Weardale road climbing out beyond the village, looking very much a true mountain road as it negotiates the deep trough of Allen Cleugh. Looking across Allendale, the cairn also makes a fine vantage point for virtually the whole walk. In contrast, behind you is an operational quarry.*

Resume on the track which leads out along the bank of Faw Side, rising a little more to gain, at this late stage, the walk's high point of some 1739ft/530m. While a short-cut down to the road may be tempting, the full route follows this through a gate and all the way to the Rookhope road visible ahead. It is joined a little short of its 1765ft/538m summit at Shorngate Cross. Advance just a few steps up it and cut across to the right to pick up a footpath descending the nearside of the wall. This faintest of trods drops down the wallside to a ladder-stile at the bottom. Continue down past a walled shaft, bearing left down to a stile to rejoin the road above Eastend Reservoir. Simply follow the road down to finish, with grassy verges alongside the plantation on your right.

Killhope Law from the currick above Byerhope

HOLMES LINN

START *Allendale Town*   *Grid ref.* **NY 837558**

DISTANCE *6³⁄4 miles (11km)*

ORDNANCE SURVEY MAPS
1:50,000
Landranger 87 - Hexham & Haltwhistle
1:25,000
Explorer OL43 - Hadrian's Wall

ACCESS *Start from the central square. Ample parking. Served by bus from Hexham.*

> *A stroll up the East Allen from Allendale Town, returning on a higher level route with outstanding views*

For more on Allendale Town, see WALK 21. Leave the square by the Whitfield road, past the Hare & Hounds and descending the steep road to the river at Bridge End. Here the East Allen is crossed by the tall, single-arched bridge. *Note the old mill in front, still proudly bearing the legend A & C Little Ltd, flour corn and cake merchants (see page 85).* Immediately across go left on a driveway running upstream. When this swings away at the end, take a bridle-gate in front to remain true to the river. Now on a bank high above it, there is evidence of recent erosion on the steep slopes below. Approaching the end of a second field the ravine becomes well wooded, and features some appreciable rocky walls at the start of Wooley Scar. The path is forced up to a stile in the corner, to resume on top of the steep wooded bank. This marks the start of a circuitous but not unpleasant detour away from the river. When the wood ends, pass through a stile to continue along the bank top to reach the start of another section of woodland.

From the stile continue outside the trees, and a little further an incoming tiny side stream forces the path along to the right. When this ends take a plank footbridge and stile in the fence and bear right across the field to a stile where fence and wall meet. Pass through an old gateway behind and resume to a length of wall on a facing corner, where a faint track is joined. Go left, over the tiny stream of Black Cleugh and away through a redundant ladder-stile/gateway and on a little further with a fence close by on the right. Don't be tempted by another redundant stile in the hedge on your right, but keep left of the hedge and a tiny side stream.

Drop down through a facing hedge, then descend the steeper bank, bearing left to a gate in the far corner of the field. A short track runs through the trees to find the cottage of Steel Wood Villa tucked away in idyllic seclusion. The path goes right outside its garden fence, quickly turning to descend steeply to the bottom of the bank. Go left along-side the Steel Burn, quickly reaching a foot-bridge to cross it just short of its confluence with the East Allen.

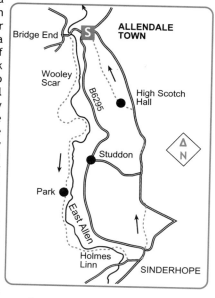

Resume upstream with the river on a colourful bank, soon reaching a footbridge on it. Don't cross unless you want a very short return, or more likely to view the river in this splendid setting. Resume along the riverbank, passing through an old wall to earn a good prospect of the substantial scar on the other bank. Bear right near the wall, noting the elaborate modern carving on a gatepost. Through an old gateway the faint path entirely forsakes the river again by rising to pass a ruin in the trees ahead. A track forms and returns you to the river under a part wooded bank, enjoying a super stroll to cross the tiny Hagg Burn to meet the grassy Studdondene-Wooley byway.

Go left over a stile to keep faith with the river, and just ahead is a bridge carrying the byway over the East Allen. Don't cross, but take a stile and continue upstream through a nice pasture. Pass through a gate and stile behind, and along the top of a little bank, with the river now beyond a wall. Continue to a stile/gate, with the riverbank looking inviting just to the left. The path however clings to the fence on the right, angling gently up from the river to a footbridge, joining a rough track ascending to the farm at Park. Through a kissing-gate in front, keep left of all buildings as you cross the side of the yard to another kissing-gate back out.

Advance on above the steeper, soon wooded bank, through another kissing-gate and then a little further to a stile into the trees. A path slants down to a footbridge: up the other side, keep left again on the field edge above a wooded bank. At the top a little bridge sends the path into a small tract of bracken, narrowing to a stile back into trees at the end. This sends the way down stone steps to cross a footbridge, and back up wooden steps to a stile out into a larger bracken tract. Bear right as indicated by a few steps, on through bracken, then more faintly on grass. The way rises more clearly again through the bracken of this broad spur, the splendid path reaching a guidepost marking a crossroads on the open brow.

Turn left, immediately back into bracken and with the path at once clear again. This time it descends through dense bracken to a stile in a fence at the bottom. Now cross a pasture to a stile back into trees. Across a small footbridge on a sidestream, the path runs upstream by the East Allen, out into a pasture, back to a wooded bank, then to a stile to the environs of an old house. Beyond it resume along the fieldside, but quickly take a stile in the fence on the left to alight surprisingly onto a footbridge high across the river. This magical moment reveals a major highlight as it makes a super viewpoint for the waterfall of Holmes Linn. *This is a truly delectable scene as the river tumbles over a broad rock barrier into a deep, dark pool.*

Across, take the path upstream above the falls and along the wood to a stone arched bridge on a sidestream. Now leave the river by a well-defined grassy way slanting up to a gate onto a back road. Turn left, rising then running along to emerge onto the B6295 at Sinderhope. *Alongside a phone box is a tiny Post office, a remarkable survivor in such a rural setting. This scattered community also features a pony trekking centre just up the hill. Just north along the main road is the former Board School of 1881, while just south is the former Methodist Chapel.*

From the junction walk north across the bridge to a cottage, then just along the side road take a small gate on the left. Ascend the steep fieldside towards the farm at East Garret's Hill, with extensive views back up the valley. Take a stile into the trees immediately left of the buildings, and rise through them to the top. Continue climbing to a ladder-stile in the wall above, then bear right up above a stand of trees to the top corner of the field. Here a short narrower way runs right, past a barn to a bridle-gate onto a road.

Go left, commencing a splendid high-level, traffic-free stride. *At around 1246ft/380m this is the summit of the walk, affording excellent views over Allendale, across to the chimneys on Dryburn Moor (see WALK 20), and north to the hills beyond Hadrian's Wall.* A gentle decline is made to the wooded enclave of Parkgates Burn, followed by a steady rise away. Just past a fine viewpoint seat, a rough road doubles back to the right. Just a little further, turn off left on the second of near adjacent drives. This runs to High Scotch Hall, just ahead. Pass right of the farm buildings, and after the last outbuilding take a wall-stile on the left rather than continuing to the house ahead. Cross to a stile in the far corner, then cross a field centre towards the house in the trees ahead, Finney Hill Green.

From a corner stile pass along the front to join the drive, just as far as the corner where it turns right. Take the stile (built into both walls) and bear left to the end of the trees just ahead. From this brow Allendale Town is revealed at your feet. Drop down the fieldside to a gateway and down again to the corner, crossing stiles straight over a driveway into the next field. Slant right to a stile in the descending wall, then cross to the far corner, dropping to a stile in the very corner. A clear path slants right to a wall-stile, then down to a snicket squeezing between the houses. Cross straight over the road and down a surfaced path to emerge back into the centre.

ALLENMILL CHIMNEYS

START *Allendale Town*   *Grid ref.* **NY 837558**

DISTANCE *7 miles (11km)*

ORDNANCE SURVEY MAPS
1:50,000
Landranger 86 - Haltwhistle & Brampton **or**
Landranger 87 - Hexham & Haltwhistle
1:25,000
Explorer OL43 - Hadrian's Wall

ACCESS *Start from the central square. Ample parking. Served by bus from Hexham.*

A hugely absorbing walk with the principal goal of tracing old lead mine flues up onto the moors. Full of industrial archaeological interest, but a grand walk even without that!

For a note on Allendale Town, see WALK 21. From the town square take the Whitfield road past the Hare & Hounds, dropping steeply down a winding bank. Before the bottom look out for an enclosed path turning off to the right, quickly entering woodland to drop down to the bank of the East Allen. This super path traces the river through woodland. By a sidestream you pass a ruined winding house from lead mining days. *Alongside, water gushes from the dark, stone arched adit of the Blackett Level, the end of a two-mile long mine drainage system.* Beyond, it leaves the woods and continues faithfully by the river to emerge at Allenmill Bridge.

Just across the river here stood the feature that created the focal point of this walk, the Allenmill smelt mill. A crucial aspect of the lead mining process was smelting, which involved heating the lead ore to produce a molten metal. The downside was the by-

product of sulphur, whose fumes were distinctly unhealthy. The problem was resolved by construction of stone flues to carry the fumes safely away. Two such flues were built from Allenmill, both well over 4000 yards long as they ascended onto Dryburn Moor to culminate in two tall chimneys. The presence of the flues unfolds as the walk progresses, concluding with the finest surviving sections on the moor itself. The mill ceased operation in 1897.

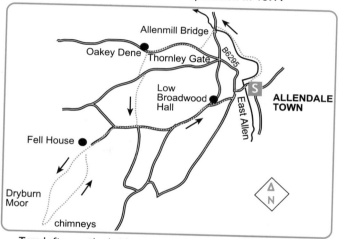

Turn left over the bridge and, ignoring an immediate path on the right, proceed just 30 paces further and after a drive take a kissing-gate on the right. A super path ascends a corner of woodland by a tiny stream. At the top is a stile, from where ascend the fieldside to a stile at the top. This deposits you onto a road just west of Thornley Gate. Turn right along here for half a mile as far as Oakey Dene. Opposite the house a path is signed up into an inviting wedge of open country. This grand path ascends through birchwood, ignoring an early branch right. Opening out onto heathery moor, the path milks this colourful little tract of country enclosing Oakeydean Burn, and at the top joins the Ninebanks road from Thornley Gate.

Turn left into the dip, then leave by a firm track ascending the wallside at the end. This climbs through heathery surrounds before easing out to run a more standard course between walls. Ahead is the taller chimney, drawing you up just like the flues. *As the flue is crossed, in evidence to your right is a 'flue fork'. They can be seen rising ahead towards the chimney standing proud on the moor.* The track, meanwhile, runs on to an unsigned crossroads by a small wood. It is to this point the walk will return.

The old flue, Dryburn Moor

Turn right, rising past the farm at Frolar Meadows to a fork, again unsigned. Go left, still ascending and now with flues evident in fields on both sides. Heathery verges take over partway up, and the tarmac ends at a cattle-grid. Advance on the continuing access road towards isolated Fell House. As it turns into the farm advance straight on the continuing track of the Carriers Way. Now the finest section begins, a super stride over grassy moor in the unfailing company of one of the flues. *Though this flue is remarkably intact, don't be tempted to walk upon it: the masonry cannot be guaranteed secure, and in any case it's a fascinating remnant of industrial archaeology.* The grassy track ascends gently and gradually enters more heathery surrounds. After drawing level with the chimney, a final pull reveals a second ruined chimney just 200 yards ahead. On reaching it both track and flue end at the summit of the walk, some 1492ft/455m on the moortop. *This squat, massive girthed chimney features twin arched entrances where both flues finally merge.*

All around is a moorland landscape, though principal focus is without doubt the taller chimney. Although you might simply return the same way, the logical route doubles back to that chimney on another flue-side track. Whichever way you go, it's all downhill! *This vantage point boasts a super prospect down-dale to Staward Gorge above Allen Banks, also to the rolling moors of Hexhamshire Common above Allendale Town.* Leave on the same track, dropping down the moor in the company of the collapsed flue. Approaching a wall at the bottom, bear left on a path back to the cattle-grid.

Retrace steps to the crossroads by the wood, this time keep straight on down the road with the town in view ahead. Merging into a wider road go left, and within half a mile a narrow back road breaks off right past Low Broadwood Hall. *The attractive farmouse bears a 1716 dated lintel.* The road drops steeply to the cluster of buildings at Bridge End to join the B6295. Turn right to the bridge on the East Allen. *On the right you pass a former tollhouse and a large old mill still sporting fine lettering.* Cross the high bridge with its single arch to finish with a steep pull back into the centre.

The old mill, Bridge End, Allendale

21

EAST ALLEN DALE

START *Allendale Town*   *Grid ref.* *NY 837558*

DISTANCE *7 miles (11km)*

ORDNANCE SURVEY MAPS
1:50,000
Landranger 86 - Haltwhistle & Brampton **or**
Landranger 87 - Hexham & Haltwhistle
1:25,000
Explorer OL43 - Hadrian's Wall

ACCESS *Start from the central square. Ample parking. Served by bus from Hexham.*

> *Easy walking in delightful surroundings above and alongside the East Allen downstream from Allendale. Can easily be halved in length by using a link path at Catton village*

Allendale is a town by name but a village in size. It is, however, capital of the Allen Dales and the focal point for residents and visitors to these lonely valleys. Built on lead mining, its population reached more than 6000 during the industry's 19th century boom years. Pretty much everything is based around the square, with tearooms outnumbered by welcoming pubs. Hidden just around the back is St Cuthbert's church, which was restored in 1873. A sundial of 1842 on the wall just before you enter shows a latitude used in evidence of the town's claim to be the geographical centre of the Kingdom, though others dispute this, including nearby Haltwhistle and Hexham; while Dunsop Bridge in Lancashire is another confident claimant, having added the associated islands to the equation. Allendale also has several shops, a bank, and a Primitive Wesleyan Chapel of 1878.

Stood at a little short of 800ft above sea level, the place has an invigorating air, and was regarded as something of a health resort in Victorian times. Today, Allendale Town is best known for its Fire Festival, a well attended New Year's Eve event. Briefly, it takes the form of local costumed men known as 'Guisers' parading around with blazing tar barrels on their heads, culminating in their deposit (the barrels, not the men) upon a large bonfire.

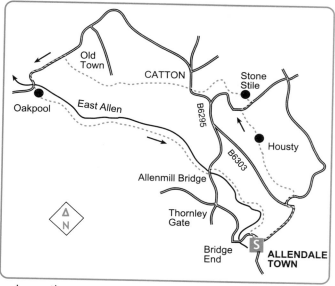

Leave the square on the B6303 Hexham road, past recreation grounds and round a sharp bend at the edge of the village. Just through it, pass a cast-iron water pump and double back sharply right up an unsigned back road. After climbing steeply it briefly levels out. Take a small gate on the left and ascend an enclosed path between gardens. At a stile at the top continue up a no-man's-land to a stile in the adjacent wall. Now slant gently left up the field. *There are good views back over the village, and across to the chimneys of the Allenmill flues (see WALK 20) on Dryburn Moor.* The pathless route crosses to a covered reservoir at a wall corner.

Continue straight on, now contouring beneath a sturdy wall with fine views down the valley. Keep on to reach a gate at the end. Advance through another unkempt no-man's-land between converging walls, turning right at the end through a gate into a field. The Hope farm stands just over to the right. Trace the wall on your left along to the far end, cross the ladder-stile and swing round the field corner towards the house at Housty. Pass left of its garden wall to a stile, then bear right to join the farm drive behind the house. Although it is simpler to follow the drive out, the map suggests that after passing a red-brick building and a stone out-house bear left on a track to a gate behind, then cross the field to a gate in the far right corner to rejoin the drive. This leads out onto a back road, with Catton village outspread across the fields ahead.

Turn right a short way, and at the first chance take a drive on the left to the farm at Stone Stile. Keep left of all buildings, taking a gate into the small windbreak of trees alongside. At the bottom a wall-stile by a barn gives escape into a large sloping field. Descend this, bearing right to a gate in the wall below, alongside a wood. Just below, turn right through another gate into what is almost an island-field enclosed by wooded gills. On the right is a substantial quarry face long since reclaimed by nature. Advance into the field and drop left, between converging gills to locate a stile in a short section of wall at the bottom. The right-hand gill (Catton Burn) is crossed by a footbridge just downstream, and out the other side turn up the wallside. Partway up the field, take a ladder-stile in the wall and make a bee-line for Catton. Another such stile is crossed then advance to a gate, from where a walled green lane leads out to a farmyard and onto the B6303 in the village centre.

Catton is an attractive village with cottages set back from a sizeable sloping green. Note that the walk can be halved by taking a path from the bottom of the green to drop down towards the river and pick up the last mile at Allenmill Bridge. Cross to the green and leave by an unsigned road between two houses by the Millennium stone seat. Past the houses the road immediately ends, and across a ford and footbridge a contrastingly grassy continuation heads off between walls. Initially shared with a small stream and at times a touch overgrown, it is nevertheless a fine way, with hints of a stone causey beneath the grass. Rising gently to steadily level out, remain on this all the way to its demise at a gate into a field, with Pasture House over to the right. At once take a gate on the left and resume on the other side of the wall to a stile at the end.

Now slant right up the pasture to a gate at the top corner, onto a farm road and path junction. Go straight across on Struthers farm drive, but leave almost at once by a kissing-gate on the right. Slant across the field, rising steadily to the far corner. Over the ladder-stile continue up the wallside, through a neat wall-stile at the top corner and resume on the other side of the wall above a steeper bank. At the end don't pass through the gate to the houses at Old Town, but curve a little left to a stile in the facing wall. Now slant down the small enclosure to a corner gate, and contour across a big sloping pasture to a stile in the wall across.

Prominent below is the course of the old railway. This is the final length of the Allendale branch that ran some 13 miles from a junction on the Newcastle-Carlisle line a mile west of Hexham. It opened in 1868 principally to serve the valley's lead mining industry, although this would already have been in terminal decline. The country through which it ran was sparsely populated, and thus the mining demise meant the line never got any further up the dale, not even the missing mile to Allendale Town. Passenger traffic ceased in 1930, but it did survive as a mineral railway for another twenty years.

Continue across to the next stile in a descending wall, on to a ladder-stile, then above a house at Staward Villa to a stile onto Colliery Lane. Turn down this very steep, narrow and part rough lane, soon passing through the course of the old railway. Continue steeply down, becoming leafy and sunken before reaching the substantial, double-arched Oakpool Bridge high above the River East Allen. Across, turn into the drive at Oakpool Farm, and on past the two houses to a gate where a cart track heads off through riverside pasture. This runs grandly on to the house at Kittygreen. Don't enter its gate, but keep left to a gate/stile. Continue across a tapering field to the riverbank. Over the stile a small section of woodland path is enjoyed, leading to a footbridge on the inflowing Crockton Burn. Just a few steps further a stile leaves the wood and you continue splendidly on the riverbank proper, across a pasture towards the renovated house at Bridge Eal.

Cross a tiny footbridge to the house, then an enclosed path runs briefly right to a stile into open pasture again. Turn left, upstream again away from the house, soon merging into its grassy drive. This super track leads on through the fine open pasture of Bishopfield Haugh. Passing through a line of trees some way beyond a stile/gate in a wall, the path leaves the track by bearing left to a stile in a fence. Across, cross to the next fence which overlooks the river. Continue with this, soon leaving the river as an old wall nudges the thin path away. Continue on, the sturdier wall pointing to the end where a kissing-gate admits into a wooded riverbank. This sends a good path on, later raking up the beech bank and on to a kissing-gate onto the B6295 alongside two-arched Allenmill Bridge.

Turn left over the bridge, and leave at once by resuming upstream on a good path. *On the opposite bank stood the smelt mill from where the extensive flues climbed to the previously seen chimneys on the moortop (see page 82).* The path remains firmly attached to the riverbank, passing several seats and sculptures to enter woodland. By a sidestream you pass a ruined winding house from lead mining days. *Alongside, water enthusiastically gushes from the dark, stone arched adit of the Blackett Level, the end of a two-mile long mine drainage system.* Ultimately the path swings left up the wooded bank to emerge onto a road on the edge of the village. Turn left uphill to quickly return to the square.

In Allendale Town

HEXHAMSHIRE COMMON

START *Allendale Town*   *Grid ref.* **NY 837558**

DISTANCE *7¹4 miles (11¹2km)*

ORDNANCE SURVEY MAPS
1:50,000
Landranger 87 - Hexham & Haltwhistle
1:25,000
Explorer OL43 - Hadrian's Wall

ACCESS *Start from the square. Ample parking. Buses from Hexham.*

> *A bracing stride across magnificent rolling moorland, with simple route-finding and wide panoramas. At its finest in late summer when the heather forms an unforgettable picture*

For a note on Allendale Town, see WALK 21. Leave the town square by crossing to the Hexham road on its south side, and turn up the side road of Lonkley Terrace opposite. This rises past the Jubilee Almshouses of 1887. *These were built in celebration of Queen Victoria's 50 years on the throne, for the use of the parish poor.* The road then leaves town, winding steeply up to give good views back before a welcome leveling out. The ascent continues again to be joined by a road from the left, where gentler climbing leads to a stand of pines on the skyline. *Looking back you have excellent views over Allendale, across to the smelt mill chimneys on Dryburn Moor, and north to the hills beyond Hadrian's Wall.* After passing The Spittal you quickly reach a byway off to the left.

Turn along this broad walled track, becoming pleasanter as heathery verges form to guide you along to its terminus at a gate onto the edge of open moorland, part of all-embracing Hexhamshire Common. Continue on the grassy track heading away, passing

Haggerstone Moss and running firmly on into splendid heather surrounds. Ignore a fork left and remain on the main way which ascends slightly then runs on to a crossroads of tracks marked by a guidepost. By now you have reached the walk's highest point, at about 1295ft/395m. *Ahead is a superb sweep of the extensive rolling moorland of Hexhamshire Common, while just up to the left a signpost stands over the pile of stones that is Stobb Cross.*

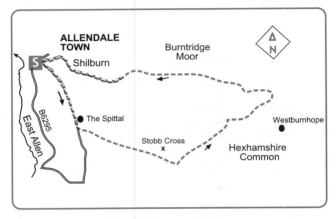

Turn left at the crossroads, now on a very clear path, rather than a track. *Looking ahead, a clear day leads the eye a long way out to the north, beyond the valley of the North Tyne to the rounded Cheviot Hills far to the north. For the next half-hour or so, you've also crossed the watershed into the gathering grounds of Devil's Water, which runs north-east to join the Tyne below Hexham.* A long, barely discernible decline through heather begins, some sections being excellent, others jaded by bridleway use. Ultimately the way merges with a wall on the right and continues down to cross the moorland stream that forms colourful Backstone Cleugh just over the wall. Up the other side the track passes an old Allendale/Hexhamshire boundary stone and resumes as before, a largely splendid walk ending at another four-way guidepost. The grassy tracts here provide an excellent spot for a break before commencing the near bee-line return across the moor to Allendale.

Turn left at the guidepost, conservatively signed 'Allendale Town 2$\frac{1}{2}$', when it's actually nearer 3 miles. So begins a similarly very gradual re-ascent over Burntridge Moor to the watershed, now on a much softer, grassy way, excellent underfoot. Crossing the marshy beginnings of Sandy Sike the way becomes firmer to reach the brow, where for a brief spell the northerly views extend for a full 180 degrees. Just beyond, the way runs straight on as the firm track undertakes a short dog-leg. The path drops back down to rejoin the track, which just beyond merge into a harsher shooters' track.

Bear left on this, soon becoming pleasanter to drop gently down rougher moorland close to a wall on the left. In the very corner a gate brings an end to the moorland crossing. A track heads away between walls, quickly merging with a surfaced driveway to commence the rapid descent back to the start, with good verges and wide views in the upper half. Simply remain on this back road all the way down, passing scattered farms and the hamlet of Shilburn to join the main road just short of the square.

Allendale from the byway onto Hexhamshire Common

WALK LOG

WALK	DATE	NOTES
1		
2		
3		
4		
5		
6		
7		
8		
9		
10		
11		
12		
13		
14		
15		
16		
17		
18		
19		
20		
21		
22		

USEFUL ADDRESSES

Ramblers' Association
2nd Floor, Camelford House, 87-89 Albert Embankment, London SE1 7BR
• 020-7339 8500

Information Centres
Alston Moor, Town Hall **Alston** CA9 3RF • 01434-382244

Railway Station, Station Rd **Haltwhistle** NE49 0AH • 01434-322002

Wentworth Car Park **Hexham** NE46 1QE • 01434-652220

Moot Hall, Market Place **Brampton** CA8 1RW • 016977-3433

Northumbria Tourist Board
Aykley Heads, Durham DH1 5UX
• 091-584 3112

Cumbria Tourist Board
Ashleigh, Holly Road, Windermere LA23 2AQ
• 015394-44444

North Pennines AONB Partnership
The Dales Centre, Castle Gardens, Stanhope, Co Durham DL13 2FJ
• 01338-528801

North Pennines Heritage Trust
Nenthead Mines Heritage Centre, Nenthead, Alston CA9 3PD
• 01434-382037

South Tynedale Railway
The Station, Alston CA9 3JB
• 01434-381696; Talking timetable • 01434-382828

The National Trust North East Regional Office
Scots' Gap, Morpeth, Northumberland NE61 4EG
• 01670-774691

Public Transport Information
Traveline • 0870 608 2608
National Rail Enquiries • 08457-484950

INDEX
walk number refers